WIND KNoT / ANATOMY OF A SNARL

INFINITY
PUBLISHING.COM

ISBN 0-7414-5290-1

Published by:

INFINITY PUBLISHING.COM

1094 New DeHaven Street, Suite 100
West Conshohocken, PA 19428-2713
Info@buybooksontheweb.com
www.buybooksontheweb.com
Toll-free (877) BUY-BOOK
Local Phone (610) 941-9999
Fax (610) 941-9959

Printed in the United States of America

Published June 2009

SONGS AND POEMS BY c y n t h i a b e r g e t

WIND KNoT /

ANATOMY OF A SNARL

One day I shall meet the man of my dreams who sees beauty in seat padding busting through seams!

Nova Pal

For Family, (including cats), friends, and Robert John Leonard

FOREWORD

("Wind Knot" ...he called it, and kindly undid the snare
knit into my fly line by mean, frisky air)

his patience, while I'm braiding, I replicate
and ne'er take scissor to misfitting plait
but six years ago naughty hair made me so blurry
that the tines of my comb must have relayed the fury
to my hair--that talked, though supposedly dead, I am skeptic
why would its knots not rise to cries of hostess apoplectic!
"Wind Knot"!..."a book title" my hair said to pursue
each sphere of hemis, chemist, angler and guru!
My anger defused, my hair has not talked since
I started that book, a page or so, my hair still makes me wince!

Six years later a light switched on in my head
MY BOOK WAS ALREADY WRITTEN!–it just hadn't been read!
So, I took to press my songs and poems of forty years history
and relax the mess-mat and tress detangler setteth free!

AUTHORS NOTES

The author may be contacted at the address below in regard to live performances of songs and poems, questions concerning musical scores and recordings, and performance rights.

CYNTHIA BERGET
(Address to be supplied later)

Frontispiece photo, "Nova Pal" taken by Beverly Jean Johnson
all other photos taken by author

INDEX TO SONGS
©2009 cynthia berget

INDEX TO POEMS
©2009 cynthia berget

Playground of beast and man
What a library for your hand!
Paint Me Montana

Serene in milken glittery court
balanced Fool Moon over Williamsport!
Fool Moon Over Williamsport

SONGS WITH GEOGRAPHY

DAKOTA DREAM

HOW I LOVE A WILD STORM
THESE MEMORIES SO VERY WARM
ARE OF A PLACE OF CHANGING SKIES
AND PROMISE OF YOUR LOVING EYES
IN MY DAKOTA DREAM I LOVE EVERYTHING I'VE SEEN

THE PRAIRIE'S FRAGRANT GENTLE KISS
IS ONE OF MANY THINGS I MISS
THE WIND AND STARS THAT FILL ONE'S SIGHT
THE LIGHTS THAT RACE THE SKIES AT NIGHT
IN MY DAKOTA DREAM I LOVE EVERYTHING I'VE SEEN

WORDS CAN'T SHOW THE THINGS I SEE
MY DREAMS OF WHERE I SOON SHALL BE
NOW, WITH YOUR LOVE I NEED NOT ROAM
MY HEART HAS FINALLY FOUND A HOME
IN MY DAKOTA DREAM I LOVE EVERYTHING I'VE SEEN

THIS LAND HAS BROUGHT YOUR LOVE TO ME
AND GRANTS THE MOST OF THIS BEAUTY
MY ONLY DREAM HAS NOW COME TRUE
SOON I SHALL BE LOVING YOU
IN MY DAKOTA DREAM I LOVE EVERYTHING I'VE SEEN

DAKOTA SKY

OH, THE DAY IS GREY, THE DAKOTA SKY
RAINS FOR ITS FIRST WEEK OF SPRING
AND THE COUNTRY WAKES WITH A WINDY SIGH
AND WAITS FOR WHAT THIS YEAR WILL BRING

RIVERS WILL FLOW FROM THE YEAR'S HEAVY SNOW
AND FOR CERTAIN, PRAIRIES WILL BE GREEN
AND GOD'S LAND IT WILL GROW FROM THE SEEDS WE HAVE SOWN
WHAT A RAINBOW OF LIFE WILL BE SEEN!

AND I LOVE THE DAY 'NEATH DAKOTA SKY
AND THE EVER CHANGING PLAINS
THE ANIMALS AND SUNFLOWERS THAT BLIND MY EYES
THE LIFE-GIVING FIELDS OF GRAINS
AND THE HONEYED STRANDS OF WHEAT THAT LAY
ON THE EARTH LIKE GOLDEN CHAINS
AND THE HONEYED STRANDS OF WHEAT THAT LAY
ON THE EARTH LIKE GOLDEN CHAINS
ON DAKOTÁ'S GOLDEN PLAINS, SOUTH DAKOTA'S GOLDEN PLAINS

FOOL MOON OVER WILLIAMSPORT

I THOUGHT YOU WERE MY PAL
HERE I AM A LONESOME GAL
FEELING SILLY LOOKING UP AT YOU
AS IF THERE'S SOMETHING YOU WOULD DO!

WAIT A MINUTE! WHAT'S THAT SMILE!
DON'T TELL ME I MUST WAIT AWHILE
PATIENCE IS FOR THOSE WHO FISH
FOR FATE TO GRANT THEIR WISH!

FOOL MOON, I THOUGHT YOU WERE MY PAL!
I'LL STROLL THE C&O CANAL
AND ASK SUN "WILL ROMANCE COME SOON?"
"GOOD IDEA." SAYS FOOL MOON

POTOMAC WINDS A LAZY CURVE
SUN SHOOTS EACH WAVE WITH DASH AND VERVE
AND WARMS MY FACE WHILE ANSWERING ME
"GO ASK FOOL MOON, MY BUDDY."

I CHECKED THE ALMANAC TO SEE
IF TONIGHT FOOL MOON WOULD BE WITH ME
TOTAL ECLIPSE AT EIGHT, IT WAS NINE NINETEEN
SLICED BEHIND SUN, FOOL MOON WAS SEEN

I'D ONLY READ OF EYES LIKE JEWELS!
LIGHT BLUE THAT BREAKS ALL HUMAN RULES
OF WHAT IS FLESH? OR WHAT IS STONE?
BLINKED AT ME THROUGH EVERY BONE!

YOU TURNED MY CHIN TO MEET OUR LIPS
FEW HOURS AFTER SUN AND MOON'S ECLIPSE
SERENE IN MILKEN GLITTERY COURT
BALANCED FOOL MOON OVER WILLIAMSPORT

AT DAWN SUN WAITED TO RELIEVE
FOOL MOON AT TASK IN MAKE-BELIEVE
WHEN HID THE LAST STAR IN DAYLIGHT
SUN SAYS, "**WILLIAMSPORT**--MOON, GREAT JOB LAST NIGHT!"

GOODBYE CALIFORNIA

GOODBYE CALIFORNIA, GOODBYE TONIGHT, TODAY
TIME WON'T BLESS A MOMENT I AM ON MY WAY
GOODBYE--HIGH, AS A TELEPHONE POLE

GOODBYE TO THE SEASHORE, GOODBYE TO THE HILL
GOODBYE TO THE MOUNTAIN, GOODBYE TO GOODWILL
FLY--WHY?

I AINT GOING NOWHERE AND THAT'S THE WAY I BE
STROLL UPON MY FOOTPRINT AND TELL ME WHAT YOU SEE
I--MY

SOMEWHERE I HAVE FALTERED I CANNOT SAY "BYE" TO YOU
CALIFORNIA AND MY FRIENDS I CANNOT YET BE THROUGH
WHY--WHY?

HOME SWEET HOME

IT'S NICE TO BE HOME WHEN NO ONE'S AROUND
I EVEN FEEL BROUGHT UP FROM THE GROUND
WHERE I CAN BE STILL AND QUIET
LIVING THE DAY AND THE NIGHT

THERE'S FIVE WINE BOTTLES ON THE FLOOR
I CAN HEAR DOGS BARKING THROUGH MY DOOR AND WALLS
I DON'T MIND AT ALL IF FREAKS COME
OR IF I LIVE IN A SLUM

THERE'S TWO FURRY KITTIES TO BRIGHTEN MY DAY
EVEN IF THEY GET IN MY WAY
AND EAT THE FLOWERS I CAREFULLY PICK
AND USE MY CLOTHES WHEN THEY GET SICK

IT'S NICE TO BE HOME WHEN BERKELEY'S AT WAR
NONE OF US KNOW WHAT WE'RE FIGHTING FOR
OH WELL, IT CAN'T BE ALL WRONG
IF IT GIVES ME A CHANCE TO WRITE A NEW SONG

THERE'S ROBBERS AND RAPISTS ALL OVER MY STREET
THE CORNERS AND ROOFTOPS ARE LOADED WITH HEAT
SOMEDAY MAN'S GONNA PAY
I WON'T CRY I JUST HOPE BY THEN I DON'T DIE

I'LL JUST SIT AT HOME AND DRINK MY BEER
AND HOPE THE REVOLUTION DON'T COME TOO NEAR
'CAUSE IF IT COMES TO THIS HOUSE OF MINE
THE GUARD WON'T LET ME OUT TO BUY MORE WINE

I GUESS I'LL STICK AROUND
I DON'T KNOW HOW TO GET OUT OF THIS TOWN
THERE'S NO PLACE BETTER THEY SAY
SOON THE WHOLE WORLD WILL LOOK LIKE L.A.!

THERE'S LOTS OF PESTICIDES IN YOUR DINNER
THERE'S SMOG ALL AROUND AND THE AIR'S GETTING THINNER
LET'S SING, WHAT WILL TOMORROW BRING
SADNESS AND MORE MADNESS

I HOPE BY NOW THAT YOU REALIZE
THAT BRICKS AND PLASTER ARE FALLING FROM THE SKIES
I HOPE YOU'RE ALL HAPPY AND DO NOT FIND
THAT YOU END UP DEAD BEFORE YOUR TIME

LADY OF SADDLE ROCK

I HAVE SEEN HER WITH THE MOON AS A HALO O'ER HER BROW
OVERLOOKING BUTTE, MONTANA, ON SADDLE ROCK SHE STANDS THERE NOW
ONE MAN'S VOW IF MARY WOULD HELP SAVE HIS WIFE THROUGH SURGERY
AND PEOPLES' FAITH, LOVE, TRUST, ADVENTURE AND DEVOTION

WITH NINETY FEET OF STEEL AND DREAMS THAT REACHED BEYOND THE SKY
FOR SOME FOLKS 'ROUND BUTTE, A COMFORT TO BE NEAR HER ALL THE TIME
AND FOR CITIZEN AND STRANGER SHE'S A GIFT FOR ALL TO VIEW
AND SHE DOES NOT FAIL TO STIR SOME EMOTION

LADY OF SADDLE ROCK ONE CAN'T MEASURE THE PRIDE!
LIVING IN THE ROCKIES ON THE CONTINENTAL DIVIDE
YOU WERE NOT MADE WITH SLAVES NOR PLUNDERS
ADD NUMBER EIGHT TO THE SEVEN WONDERS!

NOW, I GUESS, YOU'RE BOUND TO ASK WHAT SHE MEANS TO ME
SOMETIMES I FEEL JUST ONE SMALL TWINGE OF HEALTHY JEALOUSY
I'VE LOOKED TO HER THROUGH LONELY EYES BUT COULD NOT HOLD BACK A SMILE
FOR AT LEAST **ONE** GOOD WOMAN HAS BEEN HONORED WITH DEVOTION

WITH NINETY FEET OF STEEL AND DREAMS THAT REACHED BEYOND THE SKY
FOR SOME FOLKS 'ROUND BUTTE, A COMFORT TO BE NEAR HER ALL THE TIME
AND FOR CITIZEN AND STRANGER SHE'S A GIFT FOR ALL TO VIEW
AND SHE DOES NOT FAIL TO STIR SOME EMOTION

LADY OF SADDLE ROCK ONE CAN'T MEASURE THE PRIDE!
LIVING IN THE ROCKIES ON THE CONTINENTAL DIVIDE
YOU WERE NOT MADE WITH SLAVES NOR PLUNDERS
ADD NUMBER EIGHT TO THE SEVEN WONDERS!

MAIL-ORDER BRIDE (DUET)

NO, THESE AREN'T THE DAYS OF THE WILD FRONTIER
THE WEST HAS BEEN TAME FOR MANY A YEAR
BUT WILD ARE THE TOWNS WHERE A LOVE MIGHT GROW
AND THE SEARCH FOR LOVE IS DISTANT AS IN YEARS AGO

IN MONTANA WE MET, IN A BORDER TOWN
I STILL DON'T REMEMBER WRITING MY ADDRESS DOWN
NOW YOUR ARMS ARE REACHING OUT FOR ME
THROUGH UNSPOKEN WORDS, WRITTEN SO SWEETLY

I GIVE MY HEART TO YOU THROUGH THE MAIL
AND I, MY DARLING, GIVE MINE TO YOU AS WELL
WE'VE BRIDGED THE JOURNEY ONCE EVER SO WIDE
AND SOON I SHALL COME TO BE BY YOUR SIDE

YES, WE KNOW IT IS DIFFERENT AND YES, IT IS STRANGE
MAGIC HAS TOUCHED TWO HEARTS ADRIFT ON THE RANGE
YOU WOOED ME WITH WORDS, NEVER ONCE DID WE TOUCH
YET THE LOVE WE ARE FEELING IS EVER SO MUCH!

FAITH THROUGH YOUR WORDS I REDISCOVER
FOR I HAVE FOUND THE TRUEST LOVER
ACROSS THE MILES WE BURN WITH LOVE INSIDE
I SHALL FOLLOW THE FLAME TO BE YOUR MAIL-ORDER BRIDE!

YES, WE KNOW IT IS DIFFERENT AND YES, IT IS STRANGE
MAGIC HAS TOUCHED TWO HEARTS ADRIFT ON THE RANGE
YOU WOOED ME WITH WORDS, NEVER ONCE DID WE TOUCH
YET THE LOVE WE ARE FEELING IS EVER SO MUCH!

I GIVE MY HEART TO YOU THROUGH THE MAIL
AND I, MY DARLING, GIVE MINE TO YOU AS WELL
WE'VE BRIDGED THE JOURNEY ONCE EVER SO WIDE
I SHALL FOLLOW THE FLAME TO BE YOUR MAIL-ORDER BRIDE!

MESSAGE OF SPRING CREEK

WHEN A HUNGER STRIKES THE VERY CORE OF ME
AND SADNESS CHOKES THE BREATH WITH WHICH I SPEAK
WHEN MOODS LIKE THESE TEASE, TORMENT, AND DEIGN TO HAUNT ME
MY CRIES ARE GENTLED BY THE UNDERSTANDING CREEK

WHAT CLOUDS SO FRIVOLOUS IN THEIR SPLENDOURS
DRESS NATURE'S STAGE IN SHOWY CONCERT SO UNIQUE
THE SMELLS OF SUNSET AND SOUNDS AND SIGHTS OF GROWING RENDERS
THE PERFECT SETTING FOR THE MESSAGE OF SPRING CREEK!

THE CREEK IS NEVER SERIOUS
THE CREEK IS NEVER MEAN
THE CREEK IS ONLY CURIOUS
WHEN I SPILL MY TROUBLES TO ITS FLOW
AWAY AROUND THE TURN THEY GO
BURSTING CRYSTAL SHARDS OF LIGHT
ARE RIPPLES, SILVER, GOLDEN, WHITE!

YOU'VE FLESH AND BLOOD BUT NOT A CARING SPIRIT
A MIRAGE OF A MAN IS NOT WHAT I SEEK
THERE IS A VOICE TO LOVE BUT YOU'VE NOT A HEART TO HEAR IT
YOU MAY REVERE, BUT YOU DO NOT UNDERSTAND THE CREEK

NOW THERE IS A NEW WOUND DEEP INSIDE OF ME
THIS IS WORSE, I FEAR, THAN WHAT AFORE I'VE SUNG
I'VE SINCE MOVED FROM SPRING CREEK TO THE MISSOURI
AND THIS NEW PAIN IN MY HEART IS FRESHLY HUNG

THERE IS NO SPARKLING CREEK SO NEAR TO TAKE MY ANGER
AND THE MISSOURI IS TOO CLOSE TO CROWDS AND TOWN
SO I STAY INSIDE MY ROOM, NO DEAR FAMILY, I'M NOT WRAPPED IN GLOOM
THERE'S SQUIRRELS AND BIRDS AND SPRING ALL AROUND!

WHAT'S THIS! A STUDY IN HUMAN NATURE--AND I THE KEEPER!
NOW ALL I FEEL IS A WOMAN'S SHAME!
THE PAIN BEGS ME NOT TO DRIVE IT DEEPER
BUT BETRAYAL IS A SIN I'M NOT INCLINED TO NAME!

I DARE NOT THINK OF SIN WITH AN INDIFFERENCE
I WOULD LOSE MYSELF IF I WERE TO FORGIVE
EACH MORN I WAKE TO CURSE THE PAIN YOU GREED HAS CAUSED ME
I'M NOT DIVINE NOR IS MY HEART A SIEVE!

WHO ARE THEY WHO SAY THE WAY OUT IS THROUGH FORGIVENESS!
CAN IT MELT THE STRONGHOLD OF YOUR INFIDELITY?
WHILE THE PAIN BEGS ME NOT TO DRIVE IT DEEPER
A MESSAGE FROM SPRING CREEK SAYS "SEEK MY KIN, THE MISSOURI"

MONTANA MADE
I'VE TASTED THE FREEDOM OF THE WILDERNESS
AND FILLED MY LUNGS WITH LIFE'S SWEET, PRECIOUS AIR
ON TOP OF A MOUNTAIN I'VE CRIED ALL ALONE
WHEN THE BEAUTY WAS TOO MUCH TO BEAR

AND I'VE BEEN TEASED BY THE ESSENCE OF LIFE
AND NEVER HAVE CAPTURED ITS CHARMS
NOW YOUR TOUCH GIVES ME EYES TO FORESEE TOMORROW
WITH MY SOUL CRADLED IN YOUR ARMS

NOW, THE BEST TIMES AFIELD ARE WITH YOU
MONTANA MADE THIS DREAM COME TRUE
I LOVE TO GO OUT WHERE
I SMELL THE CAMP FIRE IN YOUR HAIR
OH, THE BEST TIMES AFIELD ARE WITH YOU!

A MAN NEEDS TO VISIT THE OUTDOORS
HE FINDS STRENGTH IN THE SONG OF A STREAM
THE RIVER CAN PURGE ONE OF NEEDLESS CONCERNS
AND REPLENISH THE HEART WITH A DREAM

YES, I'VE BEEN TEASED BY THE ESSENCE OF LIFE
AND NEVER **HAVE** CAPTURED ITS CHARMS
NOW YOUR TOUCH GIVES ME EYES TO FORESEE TOMORROW
WITH MY SOUL CRADLED IN YOUR ARMS

NOW, THE BEST TIMES AFIELD ARE WITH YOU
MONTANA MADE THIS DREAM COME TRUE
I LOVE TO GO OUT WHERE
I SMELL THE CAMP FIRE IN YOUR HAIR
OH, THE BEST TIMES AFIELD ARE WITH YOU!

OH, THERE'S NOTHING IN THIS WORLD I WOULD TRADE
FOR MY DREAM MONTANA MADE!

MONTANA WILL DO THE REST

WITH EAGER, PATIENT HUNGER
YOU DEVOUR HER MAJESTRY
YOUR LOVE OF HISTORY FUELS YOUR WONDER
TAMED BY YOUR CALM EXTREMITY

I'VE WARNED YOU OF MY UNFAIR ADVANTAGE
NOW YOUR HEART IS ON IT'S OWN
I AM ONLY A PART OF YOUR ROMANCING
OF THIS LAND, YOUR NEW DESIRED HOME

AND ALL I HAVE TO DO IS SMILE
AND MAKE YOU THE WELCOMED GUEST
NO WOMAN'S WEB I NEED TO STYLE
MONTANA WILL DO THE REST!

AND I DELIGHT THE WHILE YOU SAVOR
AND LEARN HOW TO LOVE A LAND
WE OWN THE CHILD'S GUILTLESS JOY
THIS MAN'S PRIMEVAL SPRIT FANNED

ON THIS FINE DAY, YOUR BIRTHDAY
WE SHARE THIS DEAR LAND AT MY REQUEST
BUT I ONLY NEED TO DO THE BIDDING
MONTANA WILL DO THE REST!

AND ALL I HAVE TO DO IS SMILE
AND MAKE YOU THE WELCOMED GUEST
NO WOMAN'S WEB I NEED TO STYLE
MONTANA WILL DO THE REST!

THIS PASSION IS ONE OF GENTLE HEALING
MEDICINE, THE MOUNTAIN STREAM
AND MAN NEEDS A SPECIAL COMFORT
FOUND ONLY IN NATURE'S DREAM

AND ALL I HAVE TO DO IS SMILE

NORTH DAKOTA, MY HOME

I'M IN NORTH DAKOTA, NEW LOVE OF MINE
YOU'VE BEEN IN MY DREAMS FOR A LONG TIME
WHEREVER I GO, I'LL ALWAYS KNOW ONE PLACE THAT'S BEEN KIND
NORTH DAKOTA, TO ME YOU ARE MY HOME

I WAS RAISED IN CALIFORNIA, I LEARNED TO GET ALONG
IF YOU CAN SURVIVE, IT SOMETIMES MAKES YOU STRONG
AND I KNOW THAT HERE IN TIME, I CAN'T GO WRONG
NORTH DAKOTA, TO ME YOU ARE MY HOME

HERE I GET TO DO THE THINGS I ALWAYS WANTED TO WHEN I WAS A CHILD
I'VE NEVER SEEN A WORLD SO TAME, AND YET, SO WILD!
THESE ARE THE DREAMS I HAD IN MY YOUTH WHEN I SMILED

AND FOR ONCE, THE STRUGGLES OF MY LIVE ARE BECOMING MILD
NORTH DAKOTA, TO ME YOU ARE MY HOME
NORTH DAKOTA, TO ME YOU ARE MY HOME

NORTH DAKOTA ROSE

THE SWEETEST KISSES ARE THOSE OF MY NORTH DAKOTA ROSE
I LOVE THOSE SOFT EYES THAT SPEAK OF THE PRAIRIE
THE ONE TO WHOM MY HEART GOES LIVES WHERE THE NORTH RED RIVER FLOWS
MY DEAREST LOVE BLOOMS IN ITS VALLEY

BUT AS I REACH FOR THIS FLOWER MY HEART CAN BE FOUND
IN THE GRASS WHERE THE PETALS HAVE SCATTERED TO THE GROUND
FOR HE GROWS IN THE PRAIRIE WITHOUT A SOUL AROUND
AND HIS HEART IS OF STONE AND BEATS NOT A SOUND

SO, I'LL GO ANOTHER MILE, I'LL EVEN STOP AWHILE
TO WATCH A ROSE SO PRETTY IN ITS BLOOMING
THEN I'LL REMEMBER YOUR KISS AND SADLY REMINISCE
THAT ONE CANNOT JUDGE A MAN BY HIS GROOMING

BUT AS I REACH FOR THIS FLOWER MY HEART CAN BE FOUND
IN THE GRASS WHERE THE PETALS HAVE SCATTERED TO THE GROUND
FOR HE GROWS IN THE PRAIRIE WITHOUT A SOUL AROUND
AND HIS HEART IS OF STONE AND BEATS NOT A SOUND
THE SWEETEST KISSES ARE THOSE OF MY NORTH DAKOTA ROSE

NOVA PAL

MY BABE WAS BORN IN NINETEEN SIXTY-NINE
IT'S TWO THOUSAND-SIX, NOVA STILL RUNS FINE
THE HEAD LINER'S GONE THE DOOR LOCK IS SHOT
MY FAMILY CAN'T KNOW THE TREASURE I'VE GOT!

I'VE BEEN LABELED "FREE SPIRIT" WITH INSULT AND PRAISE
I'LL PROBABLY BE PUNISHED ONE OF THESE DAYS
EVEN NOW, MEN RUN FROM ME--I'M A LONESOME GAL
BUT NOVA STICKS BY ME, MY TRUSTY PAL!

GREASE UNDER MY NAILS, IN THE CRACKS OF MY FINGERS
IN MY HAIRS THE SWEET SMELL OF 10W-30 LINGERS
MY EGO SWELLS WHEN I PICK UP A TOOL
FAMILY FEARS FOR ME, GUYS THINK I'M COOL!

I DREAM OF FINE PAINT JOB, INTERIOR THAT'S SWELL
YEAR AFTER YEAR FAMILY HOPES I WILL SELL
RACE CAR DRIVERS WANT NOVA I SAY "NO!"
MY FIRST CAR, MY BUDDY, GOES WHERE **I** GO!

IT'S FUNNY---MY MOST RECURRENT NIGHTMARE
NOVA IS STOLEN AND HIDDEN SOMEWHERE
I ALWAYS FIND NOVA–REPAINTED–ALTERED–SOMETIMES THE SIZE OF A **TOY**!
WHEN I WAKE FROM THIS TORMENT I'M FLOODED WITH JOY!

NOVA AND I HAVE CROSSED COUNTRY SEEN TWO OR MORE DITCH
CALIFORNIA, MONTANA, DAKOTAS, WITH TRAILER AND HITCH
ANY BREAKDOWN WAS MY FAULT, NEVER A WRECK
NOW WE'RE IN MARYLAND–WHAT THE HE_ _ CK!

ONE DAY I SHALL MEET THE MAN OF MY DREAMS
WHO SEES BEAUTY IN SEAT PADDING BUSTING THROUGH SEAMS!
UNLIKE OTHERS, WHO THINK NOVA SHOULD BE PUT DOWN
STEEL, PAINT, AND INTERIOR, WILL BRING NOVA ROUND!

SURE, I DREAM OF A FINE PAINT JOB, INTERIOR THAT'S SWELL
LIKE A WOMAN AND HER HORSE, I'VE GOT MY NOVA PAL!

PAINT ME MONTANA

PAINT ME MONTANA WITH THE LOVE THAT YOU HOLD
IN YOUR BRUSH THAT CAN NEVER GO DRY
I DON'T KNOW THE NAME OF THIS GRASS ON THE PLAINS
BUT ITS SOFT, LAMB-COLORED SHEEN THRILLS MY EYES!

BUT SOMETHING IS WRONG, FOR YOUR EYES ARE TOO SAD
DARLING, I'M AFRAID FOR MY HEART
WITH IMMINENCE OF GRIEF MY WILL CANNOT END ITS QUEST
UNTIL I'M CRUSHED BENEATH THE SHELTER OF YOUR ART!

THE SKY TODAY IS DRENCHED IN DUST COLORED CLOUDS
IT'S A PICTURE I WOULD LIKE TO RETAIN
HOW A RAINBOW OF GREY MAKES A BEAUTIFUL DAY
IN WORDS IS TOO MUCH TO EXPLAIN!

WHEN YOUR SOUL BECOMES HAPPY YOU WILL TRULY KNOW
HOW TO PAINT MONTANA AND TO LIVE ITS DREAM
A SYMPHONY OF COLOR, THIS MASTERPIECE INVITES YOU
TO BECOME TRUE BROTHER TO THE TROUT STREAM!

TALENT IS NO EXCUSE TO BE THE ARTIST BEFORE THE MAN
SUFFERING NEED NOT BE FUEL FOR INSPIRATION
WHEN YOU HAVE FREED THE ARTIST YOU WILL COME TO KNOW THE MAN
AND YOUR GREATEST WORK WILL BE IN CELEBRATION!

PAINT ME THE MOUNTAINS DRIPPED IN CREAMY WHITE
AND THE SNOW SPATTERED EVERGREEN TREES.
PLAYGROUND OF BEAST AND MAN, WHAT A LIBRARY FOR YOUR HAND!
WON'T YOU PAINT ME MONTANA, PLEASE!

ROPING THE GALLATIN

OH, THE GALLATIN, OH THE GALLATIN
ROPING THE GALLATIN
OH, THE GALLATIN, OH THE GALLATIN
ROPING THE GALLATIN

SHE IS BORN AT THE START OF THE GALLATIN RANGE
AND HEADS NORTH UP THE CANYON AND MEANDERS IN THE PLAINS
SHE MAKES A THIRD FORK WITH THE RIVERS; MADISON AND JEFFERSON
SHE SURE RUNS IN A HURRY TO JOIN IN MAKING THE MISSOURI!

OH, THE GALLATIN, OH THE GALLATIN
ROPING THE GALLATIN
OH, THE GALLATIN, OH THE GALLATIN
ROPING THE GALLATIN

HAPPY MEMORIES FOLLOW OF MY FATHER AND MY MOTHER
WHEN WE TOOK TRIPS ALONG WITH MY TWO SISTERS AND TWO BROTHERS
MY FOLKS SAID SHE IS CALLED THE "GALLOPING GALLATIN"
IS SHE GOING NORTH? SOUTH? WHERE **IS** SHE? TRYING TO FIGURE MAKES US DIZZY!

OH, THE GALLATIN, OH THE GALLATIN
ROPING THE GALLATIN
OH, THE GALLATIN, OH THE GALLATIN
ROPING THE GALLATIN

HER WATERS TURN AND RIPPLE CHURN
AND BUBBLE FROTH AND ROLL
MY LASSO IS MY EYES, MY EARS, MY NOSE, MY TOUCH, MY SOUL

OH, THE GALLATIN, OH THE GALLATIN
ROPING THE GALLATIN
OH, THE GALLATIN, OH THE GALLATIN
ROPING THE GALLATIN

SHARPSBURG PIKE COUNTRY BOY BLUES

YOU CRAVED MY INFLUENCE WITH NO INTENT FOR HABITS TO REVERSE
YOU JUST WANTED SOMEONE WHO COULDN'T MAKE YOU WORSE!
COUNTRY BOY OUT THERE ON SHARPSBURG PIKE

FIRST DEGREE, SECOND DEGREE, THIRD DEGREE LUSH
TIME BEGS YOU TO BE MINDFUL OF ITS FRANTIC RUSH
YOU THOUGHT THAT WAS CUTE, AND I SAID
THAT THE DEGREES DEPENDED ON ME, I GUESS
IT'S SO HARD NOT TO BE CRUEL WHEN YOU'RE SUCH A MESS!

I NEEDED MORE OF YOUR TIME BUT I COULDN'T LIVE IN THAT BAR
THAT'S WHERE YOUR PAIN HANGS, THAT'S WHERE YOUR FRIENDS ARE
GOT NO KISSES LAST NIGHT AT TWELVE, FELL ASLEEP ALONE AROUND NINE
IT'S NEW YEAR'S DAY, IT'S OKAY
COULD USE SOME BLUE SKY AND MORE SUNSHINE

COUNTRY BOY OUT THERE ON SHARPSBURG PIKE
WHAT WILL MY GYPSY SPIRIT LEARN NEXT TIME IT TAKES A HIKE?
IF I STOLE YOUR HEART I DIDN'T GET FAR
YOU GRABBED IT AND TOOK IT BACK TO THAT BAR!

A COUNTRY BOY DOESN'T HAVE TO TAKE CARE OF HIS HEALTH
ENOUGH BEER AND A PAYCHECK PROVIDE WORTH AND WEALTH
REINVENTION OF SELF IS OBTUSE AND "CHANGE" IS AN **UGLY** WORD
YOU LOOK AT ME BLANKLY
LIKE THIS IS SOMETHING YOU'VE ALREADY HEARD

I SAW A DIAMOND COVERED IN WRINKLES AND GLOOM
AND FELT YOUR LUNG WHEEZE IN THE BACHELOR'S DRAB ROOM
IT'S SO HARD NOT TO BE APPALLED AT THIS SOUL-WASTING SIN
I SWEAR THOSE CIGARETTES AND BEER CANS–WELD TO YOUR SKIN!

COUNTRY BOY OUT THERE ON SHARPSBURG PIKE
WHAT WILL MY GYPSY SPIRIT LEARN NEXT TIME IT TAKES A HIKE?
IF I STOLE YOUR HEART I DIDN'T GET FAR
YOU GRABBED IT AND TOOK IT BACK TO THAT BAR!

YOU CRAVED MY INFLUENCE WITH NO INTENT FOR HABITS TO REVERSE
YOU JUST WANTED SOMEONE WHO COULDN'T MAKE YOU WORSE!
I FOUND NO ANSWERS IN THAT BAR, WHAT A FINE PLACE TO SEARCH FOR CLUES!
TO THE SHARPSBURG PIKE COUNTRY BOY BLUES
COUNTRY BOY OUT THERE ON SHARPSBURG PIKE

THIRTEEN TWENTY-THREE(1323) / MOLE DANCE

WELL, I WENT TO DUMP MY GARBAGE AND ON THE DUMPSTER LID
A STICKER DISCONCERTING! WHERE WAS BIG BROTHER HID!
"NOTICE–IT IS ILLEGAL TO DISPOSE OF GARBAGE IN THIS CONTAINER AFTER
JULY 1, 1991, UNLESS IT IS PROPERLY TAGGED" —WHY SON OF A GUN!

I USED TO PICK UP LITTER LIKE A GOOD SAMARITAN
AND DEPOSIT IT IN THE NEAREST TRASH CAN
NOW, IT'S TOO HOT TO TOUCH!--I WILL NOT COMMIT A CRIME!
"ILLEGAL DUMPING" A FIVE HUNDRED DOLLAR FINE!

> WE, THE PEOPLE OF BOZEMAN, CITY'S GOT US BY THE PANTS
> "1323", DO THE MOLE DANCE
> ONE STEP BACKWARD, NOW WE'RE UNDER CONTROL
> TAKE A PEEK, LOOK AROUND, NOW--BACK TO YOUR HOLE!

"TRASH DEFECTORS" ARE GONNA HAVE TO PAY TOLLS
CITY CHARGES YOU TO GET OFF THE TAX ROLLS
PAY AT LEAST HALF OF YOUR YEARLY GARBAGE FEE
DO YOU REALLY WANT TO CHANGE TO A PRIVATE COMPANY?

> WE, THE PEOPLE OF BOZEMAN, CITY'S GOT US BY THE SHORTS
> WILL "1323" HIT THE POLICE REPORTS?
> THREE HUNDRED DOLLAR FINE FOR A DUI
> FIVE HUNDRED FOR GARBAGE–OH **MY!**

WE NEED TO RECYCLE, EVERYBODY AGREES
BUT THE CITY DOESN'T NEED TO MAKE ITS PUBLIC ENEMIES
GARBAGE ISN'T THE CONSUMER'S CREATION
GO TO THE SOURCE, PUNISH CORPORATIONS!

SUPERMARKETS USE NEEDLESS PACKAGING AND BAGS
DON'T GIVE THEM TEN PERCENT OF SALES FROM GARBAGE TAGS!
CITY!--RUN RECYCLING, AND SHOW SOME BRAVERY
REVISE YOUR POLICIES THAT PROMOTE SLAVERY!

> WE, THE PEOPLE OF BOZEMAN, CITY'S GOT US BY THE PANTS
> "1323" AND SNOW REMOVAL ORDINANCE
> HOMEOWNERS, RENTERS, EVERYBODY'S PAIN
> S I D'S UP THE YING YANG!

> WE, THE PEOPLE OF BOZEMAN, CITY'S GOT US BY THE PANTS
> "1323", DO THE MOLE DANCE
> ONE STEP BACKWARD, TAKE A RUN AROUND
> TAKE A PEEK, BUT BE MEEK–NOW BACK IN THE GROUND!

WE, THE PEOPLE OF BOZEMAN, CITY'S GOT US BY THE PANTS
"1323", DO THE MOLE DANCE
ONE STEP BACKWARD, NOW WE'RE UNDER CONTROL
TAKE A PEEK, LOOK AROUND–NOW BACK TO YOUR HOLE!

TOAST OF LEWISTOWN (THE)

WITH NO INSPIRING NAME TO BURN UPON THE POET'S TONGUE
NOR ESTATIC VIEW TO TIRE THE ARTIST'S HAND
AND ALL IS FINE WHEN NOVICE, I, A LINE HAVE CRUDELY FLUNG
CAN RETRIEVE A PRIZE INTO MY FRYING PAN!
IF THE WATER WERE A SECRET, IF THE WATER WERE A SECRET
INSTEAD OF SOME RENOWN
I'D NOT REVEAL 'LEST ONE SHOULD STEAL
THE TOAST OF LEWISTOWN!

IF BIG SPRING WERE A PERSON WE'D BLUSH AT IT'S PURITY
AND BE HUMBLED BY THE GIFTS WE CAN'T REPAY
SPRING CREEK WILL REFLECT THE TENOR OF OUR SURETY
AND GREED, THE MASTER THIEF, MUST BE PUSHED AWAY
IF THE WATER WERE A PERSON, IF THE WATER WERE A PERSON
AND ONE OF MOST RENOWN
WITH EACH MEAL I'D BE IN THE COMPANY
OF THE TOAST OF LEWISTOWN!

I HAVE SEEN BIG SPRING WHERE IT GUSHES FROM THE GROUND
DRAWING AIR TO BREATHE LIFE INTO SPRING CREEK
ON MY LAST STROLL DOWN SPRING CREEK THE BIRDS TAUGHT ME A NEW SOUND
I NOW WHISTLE BACK THE TUNE OF WHICH I SPEAK

IF THE WATER WERE A DREAM, IF THE WATER WERE A DREAM
EVERYONE WOULD WEAR A CROWN
AND NEVER WOULD COME HARM TO ROB THE CHARM
OF THE TOAST OF LEWISTOWN

IF THE WATER WERE A SECRET
IF THE WATER WERE A PERSON
IF THE WATER WERE A DREAM

TONIGHT I FELL IN LOVE WITH MARYLAND

I WISHED SO DEARLY TO FIND A HUNGER
THOUGH ROMANCE WOULD SURELY CHARGE A TOLL
BUT–OH!–IF ONLY LOVE WOULD DRAW ME UNDER
SINCE I'VE MOVED HERE I'VE SUFFERED WORSE BY FEELING DROLL

BUT, TONIGHT I FELL IN LOVE WITH MARYLAND
WHEN THE SUN COULD STILL BE SEEN IN THE SKY
THE BLUE RIDGE, A MOUNTAINOUS RUFFLE
DRESSED IN NATURE'S SMOKE-HUED MISTY EYE

THIS LAND NEVER TRIED TO GAIN MY FAVOR
NOR DID I CONSENT TO PATRONIZE
WAS PASSION, THEN, THE MISSING FLAVOR
THAT BROUGHT MY WONTS TO REALIZE?

TONIGHT I FELL IN LOVE WITH MARYLAND
WHEN THE SUN COULD STILL BE SEEN IN THE SKY
THE BLUE RIDGE A MOUNTAINOUS RUFFLE
DRESSED IN NATURE'S SMOKE-HUED MISTY EYE

WAS THIS COURTSHIP WON BY THE MAN WHO SHARED MY TABLE?
OUR WORLDS WOULD FLASH AND ARC WHILE OUR EYES DID MEET
WE DISCOVERED TO DESCEND WE WERE ABLE
AND TO BREAK THE SPIN BY GLANCING TO THE STREET

NOW I LOOK DOWN YOUR ROAD THAT I COULD DEEM AS TRAGIC
SMILING OF ADVENTURE AND NOT A BITTER THING
SPLASHED BY SUN AND SPRAYED WITH MAGIC
VIBRANT IN MY FIRST MARYLAND SPRING!

THIS LAND NEVER TRIED TO GAIN MY FAVOR
NOR DID I CONSENT TO PATRONIZE
WAS PASSION, THEN, THE MISSING FLAVOR
THAT BROUGHT MY WONTS TO REALIZE?
TONIGHT I FELL IN LOVE!

WHAT WOULD CHARLIE SAY?–"SKOOKUM ACCIACCATURA!"

CHANNING BOUGHT A HOME, A HOME ONCE OWNED BY STRAIN
HE ASKED ME TO WRITE A SONG, THUS, IS THIS REFRAIN
HE NAMED IT "CHARLIE RUSSELL MANOR" –DUE TO OPEN ANY DAY
AS A BED AND BREAKFAST, BUT WHAT WOULD CHARLIE SAY?

NOW, CHANNING PLAYS THE SQUEEZE BOX, PLAYS IT WITH SUCH ZESTS
WILL HE ISSUE FORTH A WAKE-UP CALL TO BREAKFAST TO HIS GUESTS?
HAS CHARLIE HEARD HIM PRACTICE, HELPED HIM DECORATE THE WALLS?
HAS HE HEARD CHAN TEST HIS BELLOWS IN EVERY ROOM AND ALL THE HALLS?

WHAT WOULD CHARLIE, WHAT WOULD CHARLIE SAY?
WOULD THE MUSIC MAKE HIM HAUNT US, WOULD HE JOIN UP IN THE ROMPUS?
WOULD HE SAY "I LOVE THE INSTRUMENT, WHY, EACH NOTE SOUNDS SO PURA!"
WOULD HE SAY "CHANNING HARTELIUS, "THAT'S SKOOKUM ACCIACCATURA!"

WELL, CHANNING'S GOT A BUGGY, A REAL SHINY ROLLS ROYCE
UPON REQUEST HE'LL CHAUFFEUR, TAKE GUESTS TOURING, IF THEIR CHOICE
WILL CHARLIE TELL HIS PONY, MONTE, 'BOUT THIS "SKUNK WAGON"
WILL HE ASK HIM TO TAKE HIM DOWNTOWN GREAT FALLS DRAGGIN'?

WHAT WOULD CHARLIE, WHAT WOULD CHARLIE SAY?
WHAT WOULD HE THINK OF CHANNING IN THE MANNER HIS MANOR MANNING?
WOULD HE COMPLIMENT HARTELIUS ON THE MANOR AND ITS ALLURA?
WOULD HE STAY AND HAVE A MEALIUS, LISTEN TO "SKOOKUM ACCIACCATURA"?

THE MANOR'S FRONT ROOM DONS TWO CONTROVERSIAL PAIRS OF DRAPES
WILL CHARLIE CRITIQUE THEM WHILE BREAKFASTING ON CREPES?
"I THINK THEY ARE QUITE TASTY, THOUGH YOU MAY NOT AGREE
HOW ENCHANTING OF YOU CHANNING, TO LEAVE THEM THERE FOR ME!"

WHAT WOULD CHARLIE, WHAT WOULD CHARLIE SAY?
"YOU LEFT THEM HANGING IN YOUR DOMINION JUST AWAITING MY OPINION!
WHY–THEY DEPICT THE ARTIST'S PASSION FOR FLOWERS IN VIGOROUS BLOOM!
QUICK! MY PAINTS! MY BRUSH! I'M INSPIRED, HOW THEY ACCENTUATE THE ROOM!"

WHAT WOULD CHARLIE, WHAT WOULD CHARLIE SAY?
"YOU SAY THIS FELLOW PLAYS ACCORDION TO FOLKS THAT ROOM AND BOARDION?"
WILL HE COMPLIMENT HARTELIUS ON THE MANOR AND ITS ALLURA?
WILL HE STAY AND HAVE A MEALIUS, LISTEN TO "SKOOKUM ACCIACCATURA"?

All I can think of are love songs, one ends, then one more will start
this music that I've never heard before is sung by the voice of my heart!
What Am I Thinking?

When Christmas time is here and they ask you where you will be
don't be ashamed, get used to saying "I SHALL BE HOME WITH ME!"
Christmas With Me

SONGS

AS I LIE

AS I LIE BY THE SIDE OF OPALITE DARKNESS
THE MOON SOFTLY SHINES FROM A HALO ABOVE
AND LENDS ME A KISS AND THE ARM THAT ONCE HELD ME
AND SENDS ME TO DRIFT ON A SEAFULL OF LOVE

"COME TAKE ME TO HILLSIDES" CRIES A VOICE FROM TOMORROW
"COME TAKE ME TO RIVERS" CRIES A VOICE FROM TODAY
I'LL DRINK FROM THE WATERS THEN LIE IN THE GREEN GRASS
"COME TAKE ME RIGHT NOW, I'LL SHOW YOU THE WAY"

MY FRIENDS I HAVE HEARD YOU
I KNOW YOUR CRY WELL
MY HEART IS LEFT OPEN TO WELCOME YOU IN
BUT I FEAR I HAVE LOST THE KEY TO MY CHAMBER
I FEAR I SHAN'T FIND IT 'TIL MY OWN LIFE I WIN

BLUEJAY

BLUEJAY, YOU FLY TOO LOW
YOUR SILVER DOWN DOES CATCH THE GLOW
AND IN THE DAWN
THE RIBBONS TURN TO BLUE

BLUEJAY, YOUR SONG IS SWEET
ITS SHALLOW TONE WHEN WAVES TO MEET
THE SANDY SHORE WHERE
BROKEN SHELLS ARE TRANSIENT DREAMS

BLUEJAY, YOUR CRY IS SHORN
IT ROUSES STRENGTH FROM OCEANS BORN
TO UNDERTOW YOUR MOURNFUL
CRY THAT ECHOES SOFTLY

BLUEJAY, YOUR SHADOWED TALES
CARRY OVER, HE NEVER FAILS
TO SHROUD THE SILENCE
OF WHAT WE WANT TO SEE

BROTHER

I NEVER USED TO THINK ABOUT YOU MUCH BEFORE
NOW, I THINK ABOUT YOU TEN TIMES MORE
DEAR BROTHER, WHERE ARE YOU?
WON'T I PLEASE SEE YOU AGAIN?

YOU KNOW, I DREAM ABOUT YOU AT LEAST ONCE A WEEK
AND THE WAY I FEEL, I JUST CANNOT SPEAK
THEY SAY YOU'LL BE BACK HOME AGAIN
AND THEN YOU'LL LEAVE AGAIN

I GUESS THERE'S NOTHING I CAN DO
BUT I PRAY FOR THE LIFE THAT BELONGS TO YOU
DEAR BROTHER WHERE **ARE** YOU?
WON'T I PLEASE SEE YOU AGAIN?

CHAMELEON SUN

CHAMELEON SUN
BEING OF LANGUOR
BEARING OF EARTH
COLOURING STRANGER

CHAMELEON SUN
IN RAINBOWING SPLENDOUR
PRISM OF DAY
AURORALINE BLENDER

CHARLIE'S WORLD

I'VE FOUND IT'S REALLY NOT **MY** WORLD AT ALL
YES, SOMETIMES I'M GRAND! BUT MOSTLY QUITE SMALL
I KNOW WHO HAS IT AND WHO WON'T GIVE IT TO ME
SEE HOW THE SUNS SHINES ON THE BACK OF
    CHARLIE'S WORLD–AND YOU'RE CURLED
    AND YOUR DAYS ARE DRENCHED IN KEEPING
    THOSE HOURS YOU ARE SLEEPING
    IN—CHARLIE'S WORLD I'VE TWIRLED
I'VE LAIN BY THE FIRE AND HAD ALL I DESIRE

OH, CHARLIE, YOU'RE JUST REALLY A CAT
YES, YOUR FUR IS FINE AND YOU'RE PLEASURABLY FAT
AND, I KNOW WHERE YOU SLEEP EVERY NIGHT
SOMETIMES I WISH THAT I ALWAYS MIGHT
    BE IN CHARLIE'S WORLD, IT'S NOT MINE, IT'S CHARLIE'S WORLD

CHILD (THE)

HAVEN'T SEEN YOU FOR A LONG WHILE
AND I'D LIKE YOU TO KNOW
THAT I THINK YOU CAN MAKE MY SMILE
AND MY DAY AGLOW

THERE'S A CHILD AROUND ME
WHO SPEAKS WITHIN MY EYES
WHO TAKES CARE OF JOYFULLY
LIFE AND ALL OF ITS SURPRISE

BRING HER ALONG WITH HER YOUTH
TAKE WHAT YOU CAN FIND
ASK OF NO SADNESS, MAYBE TRUTH
AND LEAVE THE REST BEHIND

AND WHEN YOU FIND THE SEASON FITTING
AND CAN NO LONGER HOLD HER HAND
IT IS ONLY THE SPRINGTIME QUITTING
AND SHE'LL UNDERSTAND

SHE WILL NOT HURT YOU
AND WISHES ONLY TO DISARM
THESE PEACEFUL MOMENTS FOR A FEW
MORE HOURS OF THIS CHARM

CHRISTMAS GROUCH / CAN I BE GONE FOR CHRISTMAS?

CAN I BE GONE FOR CHRISTMAS?
IT MEANS NOTHING DEAR TO YOU
WITHOUT ME, YOU WON'T MISS MUCH
I'LL BE GONE A WEEK OR TWO

YOU PAINT THE SUN OUT OF THE SKY
AND CAUSE THE CLOUDS TO SPOUT
YOU NEVER EVEN TELL ME WHY
RAIN FALLS INSIDE THIS HOUSE AND OUT!

I'M WEARY OF DODGING RAIN CLOUDS
THAT HOOVER O'ER YOUR SLEEVE
WHEN THEY SUSPECT A SMILE, THEY CROWD
(HAPPINESS IS NOT ALLOWED)
THEY LIVE WITH US 'TIL NEW YEAR'S EVE!

YOU'RE A GROUCH, YOU'RE STEALING CHRISTMAS
I'M ABOUT TO MAKE A DASH
YOU TAKE EACH SMILE I GIVE TO YOU
AND FLING IT IN THE TRASH!

DO YOU WISH THAT YOU WERE SOMEWHERE ELSE?
DO YOU WISH THAT YOU WERE NOT YOURSELF?
DO YOU WISH THAT YOU WERE WITH YOUR KIDS?
ARE YOU SAD BECAUSE OF THINGS YOU DIDS?
OR IS IT BECAUSE OF SOMETHING YOU DIDN'T DO?
OR WAS SOMEBODY AWFULLY MEAN TO YOU?-----**OR**

DOES **ANYTHING** AND **EVERYTHING** **MAKE YOU BLUE?**
WELL, I GUESS THERE'S NOTH----**SOMETHING** I CAN **DO!**

CAN I BE GONE FOR CHRISTMAS?
IT IS ONLY DREAR FOR YOU
WITHOUT ME, YOU WON'T MISS MUCH
I'LL BE GONE A WEEK OR TWO

YOU'RE A GROUCH–YOU'RE STEALING CHRISTMAS
YOU'RE MOODY AND YOU'RE RASH
YOU TAKE EACH SMILE I GIVE TO YOU
AND FLING IT IN THE TRASH!

CHRISTMAS WITH ME

BA, BA, **BUMP**, BUMP, **BUMP**, BUMP, **BUMP**, BUMP, **BUMP**, BUMP
CHRISTMAS WITH ME!

BA, BA, **BUMP**, BUMP, **BUMP**, BUMP, **BUMP**, BUMP, **BUMP**, BUMP
CHRISTMAS WITH ME!

WHEN CHRISTMAS TIME IS NEAR AND THEY ASK YOU
WHERE YOU WILL BE
DON'T BE ASHAMED GET USED TO SAYING
"I SHALL BE HOME WITH ME!"
IF THEY LOOK LIKE THEY'RE FEELING SORRY JUST SAY "I'M NOT BAD COMPANY!"

CHRISTMAS WITH ONE'S SELF
CAN BE AN EMOTIONAL CATASTROPHE!
YOU MAY TRY AND HIDE FROM IT, BUT CELEBRATE IN SPITE OF IT
AND GET YOURSELF A TREE!

WHEN CHRISTMAS TIME HAS GONE AND THEY ASK YOU
HOW YOU SPENT YOUR HOLIDAY
YOU CAN TELL THEM YOU WERE WITH YOUR CLOSEST FRIEND
AND CAN'T WAIT 'TIL THE SEASON COMES AGAIN
BECAUSE YOU LEARNED TO BE HAPPY AT THE TOUGHEST TIME
AND CAN'T WAIT TO HEAR MORE CHRISTMAS RHYME!

CINDERELLA AGAIN

I MUST THINK OF A GAME TO SAVE MY HEART FROM THIS PAIN
THAT GROWS FROM A DREAM OF A KISS
I MUST GO HOME

I'M CLIMBING THE STAIRCASE WITH NO FEARS AT ALL
I'LL AWAKEN ONLY WHEN I START TO FALL
OH NO!---HERE I AM
HOPING THAT I'D FOUND A FRIEND
WASTING MY TEARS AND MY PEN
ON SOMEONE I WON'T SEE AGAIN

I'M NOT CINDERELLA AT THE BALL
I HAVE NO SENSE OF TIMING AT ALL
I AM SO–ENTICED
AND FORGETTING I MUST PAY THE PRICE
FOR TRADING-OFF FLOWERS AND RICE
I'M LEFT WITH A PUMPKIN AND MICE!

I WAIT FOR A SLIPPER THAT I NEVER WORE
I'M BACK TO SWEEPING MY DREAMS OUT THE DOOR
MY FAIRY GODMOTHER HAS PASSED ME BY
AND THE ONLY THINGS REAL ARE THESE TEARS THAT I CRY!

COLOUR OF YOU EYES (THE)

IF MY SILLY HEART AND HEAD RUN AWAY
WILL YOU CATCH THEM FOR ME, AND WHAT WILL YOU SAY
IF I TELL YOU I LOVE YOU BEFORE I SEE
THE COLOUR OF YOUR EYES AND IF YOU LOVE ME

I'VE BEEN WAITING TO SEE HOW YOU WILL LOOK AT ME
AFTER HEARING THIS SONG ABOUT HOW THINGS MIGHT BE
IT JUST SHOWS HOW MY FANTASIES HAVE GONE ASTRAY
THINKING ABOUT YOU 'TIL I SEE YOU TODAY

I'VE BEEN WAITING TO SEE HOW YOU WILL LOOK AT ME
DO YOU WANT TO STAY WITH ME, OR ARE YOU ANXIOUS TO FLEE?
WHATEVER YOU DO, PLEASE, FIRST LET ME SEE
THE COLOUR OF YOUR EYES, WHATEVER THAT MIGHT BE

I'M STARTING TO FEEL LIKE HEAVEN ABOVE
I'VE BEEN CALLING MY ANGEL SO I CAN SEND HIM MY LOVE
NOW, I'M I KNOW I HAVE SCARED YOU, BUT PLEASE, FIRST LET ME SEE
THE COLOUR OF YOUR EYES–IT MEANS SO MUCH TO ME!

DEAR FOLKS

MY FOLKS ARE THE WARMTH OF THE PRAIRIE WIND
THE UNIVERSE THAT THE STARS ARE IN
THIS LOVE THAT LIGHTS THE VELVET SKIES
THEIR PERFECT LOVE DOES MIST MY EYES

IN MY LIFE WHEN LOVERS CHANGE
AND MY HEART IS WARM AND COLD
MY LOVE FOR YOU, DEAR FOLKS, WILL STAY THE SAME
THESE FEELINGS NEVER GROW OLD

IF I AM GONE FROM EARTH BEFORE YOU
AND THE LIFELINE FROM US PARTS
I SHALL HAVE YOUR LOVE FOREVER
SO, LET NOT MY LEAVING WOUND YOUR HEARTS

FALL

I'D LIKE TO RUSH THE DAY
AND HOLD IT IN MY ARMS
AND COMPLIMENT IT PERSONALLY
FOR MY RAPTURE IT ENCHARMS

OH NOW, BREAK ME APART
FROM THE THINGS I MUST NOT SEE
FOR NEVER WILL THERE BE
NAMES FOR THE DAYS THAT I BE

I HAVE SEEN TWO TREES CHANGE
FROM FROSTY GREEN TO RUST
IN MOONLIGHT GOLD, IN AFTERNOON
THEIR BENDING MAKES ME WARM

OH NOW, THE SEASON
COUNTING PAST ITS LEAVE
AND GREATLY FALL
HAS WAKENED ME

FORTRESS

I HAVE WANDERED TO A FORTRESS WHERE THE WALLS CLING TO THE SKIES
AND IT IS ONLY GUARDED BY YOUR SENTIENT EYES
LITTLE DID YOU KNOW I'VE BEEN INSIDE YOUR GARDEN
RESTING, I HAVE TRIED TO REMAIN STILL
I'VE TRIED NOT TO WAKE THE WARDEN
NOW DISPEL ME IF YOU WILL

IT SEEMS THAT I HAVE VANISHED FROM THOSE WORLDS THAT KNEW ME WELL
BUT THEY ONLY HELD THEIR TRANSIENCE LIKE A WEATHERED SHELL
LITTLE DID YOU KNOW THAT I HAVE TOUCHED YOUR FLOWERS
I'VE LAIN IN YOUR GRASS IN THE MORNING NEW
NOW I SHALL LEAVE THESE BOWERS
IF YOU WISH ME TO

THE MORNING, IT IS SWELLING, ARCHING TO BLUSH THE HOUR
I HAVE SEEN YOUR EYES UNQUELLING, SPARKLING FROM YOUR TOWER
LITTLE DID YOU KNOW THAT I HAVE STRAYED TO MEET YOU
I HAVE WATCHED YOU WHEN THE NIGHT TIME GLEAMS
I'VE BEEN WARY TO ENTREAT YOU
YOU ARE ALWAYS IN MY DREAMS

GREY LOVE

THE SUN IS GLOWING DOWN AND SO ARE ALL MY DREAMS
I'M SO USED TO WANDERING 'ROUND IN FANTASIES IT SEEMS
PLEASE TAKE ME FROM LOVE THAT IS ALWAYS DENIED
AND THE VAULT OF COLDNESS THAT I HAVE DEFIED

I FIND NO WAY TO TELL YOU WHO I REALLY AM
BESIDES, YOU'VE NOT THE AIM NOR TIME TO UNDERSTAND
CAN YOU ASK ME TO JOIN YOUR HEARTBROKEN DANCE?
I, AN INTERVAL ONLY IN YOUR SAD ROMANCE

I SLEEP IN THE ARMS OF NATURE
RESTING WHILE I ROAM
BUT I SHAN'T STAY WITH YOU
WHEN YOU'LL NOT BE MY HOME

CAN YOU ASK FOR MY HEART WHEN YOURS IS NOT TO GIVE?
IF FROM YOUR OLD LOVE YOU SHOULD PART
AM I TO BE THE SHELTER WHERE YOU LIVE?

GREY THURSDAY

I FEEL SO SAD, BUT I CANNOT TELL YOU HOW
BECAUSE EVERY TIME I WRITE A SAD SONG
I AM NEVER THROUGH

IT WAS A GREY THURSDAY
JUST LIKE THE WEEK BEFORE
IT WAS A GREY THURSDAY
HAD A GREY FRIDAY TOO
HAD A GREY SATURDAY
IT'S SUNDAY NOW, AND SUNDAY'S GREY TOO

LET ME TELL YOU, WHY I FEEL THIS WAY
LET ME TELL YOU WHY MY WHOLE WORLD IS GREY
I WOULD ONLY FEEL SO BLUE IF I WAS WITHOUT YOU
BUT I DON'T THINK I EVER HAD YOU ANYWAY
OH LORD, I'M GREY

HERE I AM AGAIN

HERE I AM AGAIN, WAITING FOR YOU
IT'S NOT THAT I HAVE NOTHING TO DO
I JUST THOUGHT IT WOULD BE NICE
I CAN'T COMPLAIN IT'LL HAPPEN AGAIN AND AGAIN

AND IT SEEMS LIKE SUCH A DRAG
EVERY TIME I'M MAD
BUT I'M REALLY JUST SAD
OH, YEAH

I COULD FILL MY TIME WITH PARTIES NIGHT AND DAY
I COULD THINK OF SEVERAL DIFFERENT KINDS OF GAMES TO PLAY
I COULD STAY AT HOME AND WISH MY TIME AWAY

AND IT SEEMS LIKE SUCH A DRAG
EVERY TIME I'M MAD
BUT I'M REALLY JUST SAD
OH, YEAH

I COULD TOY WITH SAND, BUILD A GARDEN 'ROUND MY TOWERS
I COULD FIND MYSELF BETWEEN RAINBOWS AND SHOWERS
I COULD FIND MORE FRIENDS TO WASTE AWAY MY HOURS
I COULD DRESS MY WALLS IN POLKA DOTTED FLOWERS

AND IT SEEMS LIKE SUCH A DRAG
EVERY TIME I'M MAD
BUT I'M REALLY JUST SAD
OH, YEAH

HONNIE

YOU'RE THE ONLY, ONLY ONE THAT I EVER MISS
LET ME SAY IT ONE MORE TIME
YOU'RE THE ONLY, ONLY ONE THAT I EVER MISS
I CAN SING AND MAKE MY LOVE RHYME
HONNIE, BABY, BABY

IT ISN'T VERY FUNNY, THOUGH, WHEN WE GET IN LITTLE FIGHTS
BUT BECAUSE WE LIKE EACH OTHER WE CAN ALWAYS MAKE THINGS RIGHT

IT ALWAYS MAKES MY DAY TO KNOW THAT YOU LIKE ME SO
MORNING, AFTERNOON AND EVENING
WITH YOU ALWAYS, THAT I KNOW
HONNIE, BABY, BABY

HOW ARE YOU DOING TODAY?

HOW ARE YOU DOING TODAY? I SAY I'M DOING FINE
THERE IS SOMETHING I MUST TELL YOU, I JUST CAME HERE TO PASS THE TIME
YOU SAY YOU HAVE COMPASSION THAT I WILL GAIN SOMEDAY
BUT CAN YOU LOVE A MAN WHO ROBS YOU OR STANDS IN YOUR WAY?

WHAT MAN DOES NOT LOVE A PRETTY GIRL WHEN SHE'S LOST AND CONFUSED
LET ME TELL YOU, LOVE NOT THE ONE WHOM YOU TEND TO CHOOSE
IF YOU THINK YOU ARE A BETTER MAN, THEN I TELL YOU WILL LOSE!
I KNOW I'M SELFISH, BUT I'M TRYING TO GIVE YOU THE CLUES

LOVE HE WHO WOULD DESTROY YOU, IT IS THE HARDEST THING TO DO
LET THERE BE NO MAN TO WHOM YOU CANNOT SAY "I LOVE YOU"
I TELL YOU I AM ANGRY FOR BEING SUCH A FOOL
FIRST YOU MUST LOVE YOURSELF, IT IS THE ONLY TOOL

EVERY TIME MAN IS BORN HE IS ANGRY ONCE AGAIN
GIVING IN TO A GUILT HE FEELS MUST LAST HIM TO AN END
HE IS UNGIVING AND HE DOES NOT UNDERSTAND

HOW ARE YOU DOING TODAY? I SAY I'M DOING FINE
THERE IS SOMETHING I MUST TELL YOU, I JUST CAME HERE TO PASS THE TIME
YOU SAY YOU HAVE COMPASSION THAT I WILL GAIN SOMEDAY
BUT CAN YOU LOVE A MAN WHO ROBS YOU OR STANDS IN YOUR WAY?

I DON'T BELIEVE IN LONELINESS

EVENING CHILLS THE SKY
I WONDER WHY I'M LONELY
WHEN YOU'RE GONE HOURS ARE LONG
I WISH THAT I COULD ONLY

KNOW THAT LONELINESS IS WHAT WE USE TO PUT IN DIFFERENT PLACES
WE SAVE SO DEAR, OUR MEASURED FEAR TO FILL IN EMPTY SPACES
I DON'T BELIEVE IN LONELINESS

I'M NOT GOING TO WAIT, I KNOW IT'S TOO LATE
YOU WON'T BE BACK TONIGHT
I DON'T REALLY DARE TO SAY I DON'T CARE
SOME DAY I WISH I MIGHT

KNOW THAT LONELINESS IS WHAT WE USE TO PUT IN DIFFERENT PLACES
WE SAVE SO DEAR, OUR MEASURED FEAR TO FILL IN EMPTY SPACES
I DON'T BELIEVE IN LONELINESS

WHAT AM I TO DO, I THINK ABOUT YOU
I KNOW I UNDERSTAND
I'M STILL SAD BUT IT'S TOO BAD
YOU KNOW, THIS LIFE IS NOT THE WAY I PLANNED

I DON'T BELIEVE IN LONELINESS
I DON'T BELIEVE IN LONELINESS
I DON'T BELIEVE IN LONELINESS

I'D BE ROAMING

YOU ASKED ME WHAT I'D DO IF I DID NOT DEPEND ON YOU
I DIDN'T TELL YOU, BUT I'D BE ROAMING
I SAID "IT'S NOT FOR YOU TO ASK ME TO PREDICT FATE'S TASK!"
BUT I'D BE ROAMING
YOU SHOULD NOT HAVE BEEN SO HEARTLESS, I TOLD YOU I WAS DOWN
AND NOW I'VE STARTED FEELING AS IF YOU'RE NOT AROUND

YOU ASKED ME WHAT I'D DO IF I DID NOT DEPEND ON YOU
I'D BE SINGING, I'D BE SINGING
IS IT WORTH THE WEARY CHASE TO FILL A LONELY SPACE?
I WOULD BE SINGING
YOUR INQUIRY HAS A BURN TO IT, TO IT, A STING OF FROST
NOW, I SEARCH THE WHEREABOUTS OF THOSE DREAMS I'VE TOSSED

SAD PHRASES ONLY COULD I WRITE SINCE I MET YOU
HOPE CENSORED ALL MELODIES OF UNHAPPINESS I KNEW
I HAD NOT THE BALM OF MUSIC TO TAKE THE PAIN FROM ME
FOR SORROW, AS JOY, NEEDS EXPRESSION TO OWN A SPIRIT FREE

AND **HOPE** BUILT A DAMN WHERE IT COULD GUARD AND DISAPPROVE
ACTIONS FROM MY HEART AND MOURNFUL SONGS THAT DARED TO MOVE
CONCERNING **MELODIES** IT WAS SUCCESSFUL IN ITS QUELL
THOUGH INK, NOR PEN, NOR PAPER STRUGGLED BENEATH ITS SPELL

THIS STAGNANT DAMN THAT COULD ONLY FILL A BITTER ME
HAS CRACKED BENEATH YOUR CALLOUS WORDS AND SET ALL MUSIC FREE
TWO YEARS' SUSPENSION IN A NOTEBOOK, A CRUEL AND SHAMELESS CRIME!
MY WORDS RECLAIM THE VOICE TO SING THEIR STORY OF HAPLESS RHYME!

I LIKE TO GO A'WALKING

I LIKE TO GO A'WALKING, AND IT WILL SETTLE
AND THOSE TIMES ARE NOT SO TROUBLED THEY ARE NOT DARKENED
AND YOU ARE A REFUGE SO THAT I NEED NOT HIDE AWAY
AND I THINK THAT IN MY DELUGE I SHALL STAY

AND MY WAYS ARE QUIET, AND THEY WILL SETTLE
AND MY DREAMS ARE NOW CONTINUED THEY ARE NOT TWISTED
AND YOU ARE A REFUGE AND MY NEEDS NOT MUCH CHANGE
THE WAYS OF A RECLUSE I LEARNED WERE STRANGE

I LIKE TO GO A'WALKING, AND IT WILL SETTLE
WHEN YOUR MEMORY COMMANDED YOU ARE BROKEN
AND YOU ARE A REFUGE AGAIN MY THOUGHTS ARE CLEAR
I HOPED THAT MY MUSE WOULD BRING ME HERE

I MUST FEEL

I MUST FEEL FOR TONIGHT
FOR TOMORROW MAY NEVER COME
I MUST FEEL FOR THE DARKNESS TOO
'CAUSE MAYBE SOMEDAY I'LL MISS THE SUN
    AND FOR THE DAYS I'VE MISSED YOU SO
    I WOULD NOT LET YOU OUT OF MY MIND
    WE MUST NOT LET ALL PURPOSE FADE
    OR LEAVE OUR LOVES BEHIND

I MUST FEEL FOR TONIGHT
FOR TOMORROW I MAY NOT AT ALL
IF WE DO NOT WEEP FOR THE MOMENT
NO MORE RAIN WILL FALL
    AND FOR THE DAYS I'VE MISSED YOU SO
    I WOULD NOT LET YOU OUT OF MY MIND
    WE MUST NOT LET ALL PURPOSE FADE
    OR LEAVE OUR LOVES BEHIND

I MUST FEEL FOR TONIGHT
FOR DAWN WILL COME AGAIN
AND, OH LORD, I HOPE I'M READY
READY FOR THE TIME MY LIFE WILL END

I'M NOT MYSELF

I TRY MY BEST TO COVER
THE THINGS THAT I ALWAYS DISCOVER
I'M TRYING TO FIND OUT WHEN I CAN BE MYSELF AGAIN
AND MORNING LENDS ANOTHER PLEASANT DAY

THE QUESTION THAT I TRY TO HIDE
IS HAPPINESS BEST ON THE OUTSIDE?
NOW THAT I AM NICER NOW STILL I CANNOT FIGURE HOW
I HAVE ANY PROBLEMS AT ALL

I ALWAYS COMPETE
WITH THE MAN WHO SAYS HE'S COMPLETE
I JUST HOPE YOU LOVE ME 'TIL I HAVE NOT TO FIGHT MY WILL
KEEP ME 'TIL TOMORROW AFTERNOON
AND I HOPE IT WILL BE SOON

EVERYBODY TELLS ME I AM WRONG
THAT IS WHY I SING THIS SONG
KEEP ME 'TIL TOMORROW AFTERNOON
AND I HOPE IT WILL BE SOON

I'VE BEEN THINKING

I'VE BEEN THINKING
ABOUT THE THINGS I THOUGHT I SHOULDN'T THINK ABOUT
THEY ARE A MIRROR AND RETURN TO ME WHEN I'M UNTRUE
AND I THINK ABOUT YOU

I MAY GO AWAY
YOU ARE WITH ME ALWAYS, ALWAYS WITH ME YOU REMAIN
I HAVE REMOVED MYSELF TO LEARN TO LIVE THE WAY I FEEL
AND I AM REAL

I'VE BEEN THINKING
ABOUT THE THINGS I THOUGHT I SHOULDN'T THINK ABOUT
THEY ARE UNCOUNTED AND RETURN TO ME WHEN I'M UNTRUE
AND I THINK ABOUT YOU

JUST ANOTHER ROSE

I MUST HAVE KNOWN WHEN I WAS YOUNGER
THAT I WOULD WALK ALONE
MY WALKS BECAME A PART OF ME
AND I HAD THE NEED TO ROAM

SO WHAT!--IF OUR LOVE DOESN'T WORK
IT MATTERS NOT TO ME
YOU'RE JUST ANOTHER ROSE THAT'S DIED
ON THE PRAIRIE

A MAN TO ME, IS A SONG TO WRITE
AND WILL MAKE MY HEART SAD
AND I'LL ALWAYS FIND NEW TEARS TO SPILL
OVER A LOVE I NEVER HAD

MY TRUE LOVE WILL BE THE AIR I BREATHE
AND HE WILL SHARE MY WALKS WITH ME
HE'LL NOT BE JUST ANOTHER ROSE THAT'S DIED
ON THE PRAIRIE

JUST AS LONELY

NOW THAT YOU'RE BACK IN MY LIFE
IT'S STILL GOING TO BE THE SAME
NOW THAT YOU'RE HERE, IT MAKES SOME THINGS CLEAR
BUT I 'AINT GOING TO PLAY THOSE GAMES

I'M SO GLAD TO HAVE YOU
AND TO HOLD YOU ONCE AGAIN
BUT I'M STILL JUST AS LONELY AS BEFORE

NOW THAT YOU'RE BACK, MY LOVE
I CAN GET SOME SATISFACTION
BUT TO FIND ANOTHER ONE'S MIND
I'M NOT SURE MY REACTION

I'M SO GLAD TO HAVE YOU
BUT STILL I'VE GOT THESE CHAINS
I'M SO GLAD TO HAVE YOU
BUT SOME THINGS DO REMAIN

I'M STILL JUST AS LONELY
I'M STILL JUST AS LONELY
I'M STILL JUST AS LONELY AS BEFORE

LIFE I PLANNED (THE)

I AM JUST BEGINNING THE LIFE I FASHIONED YEARS AGO
I NOW REALIZE AS I LIVE THE DREAM
YOU HAVE SHOWN ME THE WAY I THOUGHT YOU COULD NEVER KNOW
YOU HAVE DANCED INTO MY SPIRIT
NO, NO, I DON'T WANT TO GO ON KNOWING THAT MY LIFE IS PLANNED

TOMORROW I HOPE TO FEEL DIFFERENTLY
BUT WHAT WILL HAPPEN IS WHAT I KNEW I WOULD SEE
AND EACH DAY I DON'T SEEM TO BE QUITE FREE
CAN YOU BELIEVE IN MY EYES MY LIFE IS ONE BIG DISGUISE
WHO KNOWS WHAT LIES FILL OUR HEADS EVERY DAY
NO, NO, I DON'T WANT TO GO ON KNOWING THAT MY LIFE IS PLANNED

LONELY BOOTS

THESE BOOTS THAT I STRAYED OUT IN THE RAIN IN
BROUGHT ME UP THE STAIRS TO YOUR DOOR
I PUT THEM ON TO LEAVE YOUR APARTMENT
AND THEY LED ME BACK TO MY LONELINESS ONCE MORE

THESE LONELY BOOTS THAT I PUT IN THE CLOSET
THEY ARE DAMPENED BY THE RAIN
I DON'T KNOW WHERE NEXT THEY WILL LEAD ME
BUT NEVER TO YOU AGAIN

WHEN I WOKE UP THIS MORNING
I WAS STILL LOST IN MY DREAMS
MAYBE I WAS JUST CONFUSED
ABOUT TOO MANY THINGS

I WENT INTO THE CLOSET
MY BOOTS WERE LYING THERE
THEY HAD DRIED DURING MY SLUMBERS
WAITING TO LEAD ME TO SOMEWHERE

LOVE LULLABY

ACROSS A WIDE EXPANSE YOU HAVE TAKEN ME
YOU HOLD MY HAND, I NEED NOT SEE
THERE IS NO ENDLESS DROP BELOW
I FLOAT ON AIR IN A TIMELESS GLOW

MAY IT BE AGE THAT HAS TAUGHT ME SO
THAT LETS ME PASS IN WORLDS THAT I DON'T KNOW
I LINGER IN AND OUT OF TIME
I AM CRADLED IN AN ENDLESS RHYME

YOUR FIRST KISS TO ME WAS GOLDEN RAIN
A TENDER TREASURE I CAN'T EXPLAIN
SO WARM AND SWEET, IT WILL ALWAYS BE
A GENTLE TUNE DEEP INSIDE OF ME

AND IF A JEWEL THAT YOU CAN LIVE
A SONG TO YOU IS WHAT I'LL GIVE
A LOVE LULLABY SO RICH AND FULL
THAT IT SPARKLES CLEAN WITHIN YOUR SOUL

A LOVE LULLABY WITHIN YOUR SOUL

MAYBE I WILL KNOW YOU

I COME FOR YOU IN DARKEST NIGHT
MY LOVE, I COME TO HOLD YOU TIGHT
ALTHOUGH, I KNOW THAT LOVE CAN ONLY HELP
TO FIND A WAY TO BE FREE SOMEDAY
MAYBE I WILL KNOW YOU
AND MAYBE YOU WILL KNOW ME TOO

I CAN'T BELIEVE THE WAY I FEEL
CAN ALL THIS HAPPINESS BE FOR REAL?
BEFORE, THE DOOR WAS IN MY WAY AND I COULD NOT SEE
WHAT WAS INSIDE OF ME
MAYBE I WILL KNOW YOU, AND MAYBE YOU WILL KNOW ME TOO

WHY DON'T WE NOTICE WHEN WE ARE GLAD?
WE ONLY SPEAK OF TIMES WHEN SAD
SOMEHOW, ALLOW YOURSELF TO FIND A WAY TO REALLY LIVE
YOU KNOW HOW TO GIVE
MAYBE I WILL KNOW YOU, AND MAYBE YOU WILL KNOW ME TOO

MY GARDEN

DON'T LIKE SCARY MOVIES NO MORE DON'T LIKE TO GET TOO DRUNK
DON'T WANT TO PUT DOWN MY FRIENDS NO MORE, JUST WANT TO BE CONTENT
SO I'LL WORK IN MY GARDEN DAY BY DAY
AND HOPE NOTHING COMES AND TAKES IT AWAY
'CAUSE MY POPPIES AND CORN JUST BEGUN TO GROW
AND IT KEEPS ME FROM BEING LOW

SO TURN OFF THAT OLD TV, I MUST REST MY HEAD
DON'T WANT NO MONSTERS TO DISTURB MY BED
SO TURN OFF THAT OLD TV, I'VE HAD A HARD DAY
JUST TRYING TO WISH MY DEVIL AWAY

DON'T LIKE SCARY MOVIES NO MORE DON'T LIKE TO GET TOO DRUNK
DON'T WANT TO PUT DOWN MY FRIENDS NO MORE, JUST WANT TO BE CONTENT
SO I'LL WORK IN MY GARDEN DAY BY DAY
AND HOPE NOTHING COMES AND TAKES IT AWAY
'CAUSE MY POPPIES AND CORN JUST BEGUN TO GROW
AND IT KEEPS ME FROM BEING LOW!

NATURE'S SWEETHEART

NO SWEETHEART HAVE I, YET I AM NOT BLUE
YES I AM! BUT I'M NOT! YES I DON'T! BUT I DO!
I'M ALONE, YES, AND **HAPPY!** HOW CAN THIS BE?
YO DEE, OH DEE, OLODDLE DEE!
NO BURSTING OF POEMS TO WEAR OUT MY PEN
NO FLIP FLOPPING HEART TO BREAK ONCE AGAIN
NO SECRET SMILE SOMEONE'S WEARING FOR ME
NO ONE'S SHARING WITH ME NO ONE'S CARING FOR ME

I STEP OUTSIDE OF SADNESS TO TRY OUT MY TRICK
AND PLUNGE INTO NATURE WHEN TROUBLES ARE THICK
THE PERFECT LOVER IS WAITING FOR ME
YO DEE, OH DEE, OLODDLE DEE!

A THEATRE OF BEAUTY EXPLODES IN THE SKIES
ADVENTURES TO DRINK IN WITH FRESH GREEDY EYES
ADORED BY THE SUN'S SPLENDOROUS WARMTH I'M RENEWED
I AM WOMANHOOD WOOED I AM IN A FINE MOOD!

BUNDLED IN JOY I'M TRANSPORTED TO WHERE
TROUBLES ARE BUBBLES WHEN TOSSED TO THE AIR
BUBBLES MAKE RAINBOWS TO CLIMB RUNG BY RUNG
AND POP WHEN I LAUGH! DANCE! STICK OUT MY TONGUE!

THE ARMS OF NATURE TAKE FROM ME EACH CARE
THE SWEET WIND STEALS KISSES AND FLIRTS WITH MY HAIR
THE SUN CUDDLES MY BODY THE GRASS TICKLES MY TOES
YO DEE, OH DEE, OLODDLE DEE!

I AM THOROUGHLY EXHAUSTED, FULFILLED AND REFRESHED
MY POOR HEART IS HEALING AND LOVE'S WOUNDS REDRESSED
I AM PLACED ON A PEDESTAL WHERE NO MAN CAN OFFEND
I AM NATURE'S SWEETHEART, AND LOVER, AND FRIEND!

NIGHT OWL

LIQUID PEARL, A TEAR FROM THE EYES OF NIGHT
MANY OF THE REAL CAUGHT IN A WEB OF SIGHT
SHADOWS HAVE CROSSED THE LINE
HEAVY IS THE CHAIN OF TIME

NIGHT OWL YOUR CALL IS FORBIDDEN
NIGHT OWL THE PATH IS WELL-HIDDEN
LOVE ME, LOVE ME, LOVE ME

RESTLESS DAYS WRAP THEIR SUN IN GREYEST HUNGER
FEAR THE NIGHT CHILD, HATE WILL DO YOU UNDER
SHADOWS HAVE CROSSED THE LINE
HEAVY IS THE CHAIN OF TIME

NIGHT OWL YOUR CALL IS FORBIDDEN
NIGHT OWL THE PATH IS WELL-HIDDEN
LOVE ME, LOVE ME, LOVE ME

NIGHT OWL WITH EYES SHINING BRIGHT
LOVE ME THROUGH THIS
NIGHT---OWL THE MOON IS FALLING
NIGHT OWL I HEAR YOU CALLING

NOTHING'S HAPPENING

IT'S NOT THAT NOTHING'S HAPPENING
MY LIFE IS NOT AT EASE
I USED TO WRITE MORE FREELY
I HAD MORE WORDS THAN THESE

I'VE WANTED TO SAY "I LOVE YOU"
SO MANY TIMES BEFORE
BUT IF I HAD THE WORDS TO SAY IT
I'D HAVE TO THINK OF MORE
MAYBE I'VE STOPPED BREATHING
MAYBE I'M LIVING AND NOT FEELING

DON'T KNOW WHAT I'M DOING
I JUST KNOW ONE THING
WHAT I LIKE TO DO BEST
AND THAT IS TO SING

BUT I TRY TO FORGET IT
'CAUSE IT'S HARD SOMETIMES
TO SAY WHAT YOU MEAN
AND MAKE UP RHYMES

OH, I WISH I HAD A BOTTLE OF BEER

OH, I WISH I HAD A BOTTLE OF BEER
OH, I WISH I HAD A BOTTLE OF BEER
IT WOULD BE JUST FINE
IF I HAD A BOTTLE OF WINE

YOU SAID YOU WOULD LIKE MARY JANE
WOULD YOU LIKE HER PRETTY OR WOULD YOU LIKE HER PLAIN?
YOU DON'T CARE WHAT SHE LOOKS LIKE, AND DON'T ASK YOU WHY
JUST AS LONG AS SHE CAN GET YOU HIGH

I LIKE MY HOT DOGS BURNT ALL AROUND
THEY'RE GOOD DIPPED IN ASHES THAT TOO, I HAVE FOUND
MOST PEOPLE LIKE THEIRS COOKED GOLD AND BROWNED
BUT I LIKE MINE BEST WHEN THEY TASTE LIKE THEY'VE BEEN DROPPED ON THE GROUND

OH, I WISH I HAD A BOTTLE OF BEER
OH, I WISH I HAD A BOTTLE OF BEER
OH, IF I HAD A BOTTLE OF WINE
BET YOU I'D DRINK IT IN NO TIME

OH, ME

OH ME, OH MY, I WISH THAT I WAS BY THE SEA, OH SIGH
IT WOULD FILL ME UP WITH SUCH GLEE, OH WHY,
WHY AM I NOT WHERE I'M SUPPOSED TO BE?

DON'T PUT ME DOWN IN THE MORNINGS WHEN I'M HAPPY
SING A SONG TO JASMINE AND TO LEMON TREE, MY LOVES
I HAD A DREAM LAST NIGHT, HOW LOVELY IS THE CORN
AND I HOPE THAT I SHALL ALWAYS SING WHEN I WAKE UP EVERY MORN

OH ME, OH MY, I WISH THAT I WAS ON A HILL, OH SIGH
MY ONLY WISH IS THAT I CAN BE STILL, OH, WHY
WHY IS IT THAT I AM NOT YET FREE?

DON'T PUT ME DOWN IN THE MORNINGS WHEN I'M HAPPY
RESTLESS ARE THE CITY SLEEPERS TORN BETWEEN THE SUN
I HAD A DREAM LAST NIGHT, HOW LOVELY ARE YOUR EYES
AND I HOPE THAT I SHALL ALWAYS SING AS I LOOK INTO THE SKIES

PLEASE FORGET ME

IF THERE'S THINGS I WANT TO TALK OF I HAVE NOTHING REAL TO SAY
AND IF I TRY THE CONVERSATION IT'S JUST ANOTHER GAME I PLAY
I WISH SOMEDAY I'D SHUT MY MOUTH AND LOVE ANOTHER DAY
PLEASE FORGET ME, PLEASE DON'T LET ME

I WISH, I WISH, I WAS THE SUN NO FEAR I SHALL BE BURNED
I DON'T SEEM TO MAKE HEADWAY ON ALL THAT I HAVE LEARNED
AND WHAT EVER HAPPENS NEXT I SHOULD NOT BE CONCERNED
PLEASE FORGET ME, PLEASE DON'T LET ME

WINTER DOES NOT ASK YOU
SPRINGTIME FILLS YOUR HAND
SUMMER WILL FORGET YOU
FALL LEAVES YOU WHERE YOU STAND
PLEASE FORGET ME, PLEASE DON'T LET ME

PRAIRIE WIND

LONELY AS THE PRAIRIE WIND
SWEEPING O'ER THE PLAINS
MOVING CLOUDS ACROSS MY HEART
BLOWING IN THE RAINS

ONE DAY I SHALL BE AS COLD AS THE DEEPEST SEA
AND MY HEART WILL BE LOST TO EVEN ME

LONELY AS THE CLEAREST SKY
FILLED WITH STARS SO BRIGHT
LONELY AS THE STILLEST EARTH
THAT I STAND UPON TONIGHT

ONE DAY I SHALL BE AS COLD AS THE DEEPEST SEA
AND MY HEART WILL BE LOST TO EVEN ME

I REMEMBER THOSE EYES THAT WOULD NEVER CARE
THOSE EMPTY EYES THAT PUT TEARS IN MINE
I'M NOT LOST, IT'S JUST THAT THE PRAIRIE WIND
IS THE ONLY FRIEND THAT I CAN FIND

SOMEDAY WHEN WE MEET AGAIN
YOU'LL TELL ME THAT YOU CARE
YOU'LL SEARCH IN MY EYES FOR THE LOVE I HAD
TO FIND THE PRAIRIE WIND LIVES THERE

RESTLESS SHADOW

NIGHT GROWS WITH STRANGE DELIGHT
AND OFFERS RIDDLES TO MY SIGHT
LET US DO ALL THAT WE MIGHT
SHADOWS FALL WHEN COMES THE LIGHT

SUN SMILES WITH GENTLE GLEAM
AS TIME WILL PASS IN STEADY STREAM
CAN YOU HEAR SOMEONE SCREAM?
WHAT YOU KNEW IS WHAT YOU'VE SEEN

A RESTLESS SHADOW WAITS BY DAY
TO LIVE EACH TUNE THAT HE WILL PLAY
AND SING EACH WORD THAT HE WILL SAY
WHEN NIGHT COMES, HE'LL NOT FADE AWAY
AND STRUGGLING IN THE TASTE OF LIFE, EACH LIE CONCEALS A HIDDEN KNIFE

SEAGULLS ON THE PLAIN

THE SUN, IT IS LOWING
THREE SEAGULLS LOST ON THE PLAIN
THE SKY EASES DOWN ITS LEAD CURTAIN
AND HASTENS THE DAYLIGHT TO WANE

THREE SEAGULLS, TO WHERE ARE YOU GOING?
WEST LIES THE SHORES TO THE SEA
YOU NEED TO REFRESH YOUR BLUE PALLOR
AS ITS VESSELS YOUR PASSAGE IS FREE

THE SHELF OF THE SKY IT IS SHIFTING
AND HANGS AS A STEP TO YOUR LAND
MAY IT BE THAT YOUR FLIGHT IS UPLIFTING
OR YOUR BLOOD IT WILL TURN TO SAND

THE SUN, IT IS LOWING
THREE SEAGULLS LOST ON THE PLAIN
MAY IT BE THAT YOUR SHIPS ARE WELL-FAVORED
YOUR BLUE PALLOR YOU NEED TO REGAIN

SEE

OH, MY KNIGHT, HE WILL COME PRANCING ON HIS HORSE UNTO THE SEA
AND WHISPER AS THE WHITE FOAM KINDLY SPLASHES ON HIS KNEE
OCEAN, OH SEE, OCEAN, OH SEA

OH, THE SUN MY EYES DOES CAPTURE, BIND ME TO THE STEELY WAVE
I DREAM WITHIN A CIRCLE MY STREETS IN SPIRAL PAVE
OCEAN, OH SEE, OCEAN, OH SEA, A SYMPHONY FOR ME

OH, MY KNIGHT HE WILL COME PRANCING ON HIS HORSE UNTO THE SEA
AND WHISPER AS THE WHITE FOAM KINDLY SPLASHES ON HIS KNEE
OCEAN, OH SEE, OCEAN, OH SEA

SOLDIER

THERE IS NO MAN THAT I OWE TO
FOR NO MAN'S SORROW SHALL I PAY
BRIGHTEN MY WORLD WITH A FRESH START, LAUGHING, LOVING
I HAVE NO USE FOR A TORN HEART, LEAVE ME, LONGING
IF YOU CAN'T GIVE ME A NEW PART
LEAVE ME NOW FOREVERMORE

ENDLESS NIGHTS WE HAD CAPTURED
BLESSED BY THE HALT OF TIME
WE HELD THE DAYS IN THEIR FAWNING, LAUGHING, LOVING

WE HAD THE MOON AND SUN YAWNING, BREATHLESS, RESTLESS
SOON TIME, DISTENDED WAS DAWNING
LOVE ME NOW OR NEVERMORE

IF YOU WANT ME YOU MUST FIND ME
I AM NOT HERE AT YOUR CALL
IF YOU FIND ME SO INVITING–LOVE ME, HOLD ME
BUT IF LOVE IS TOO EXCITING–LEAVE ME, LONGING
I WON'T BE THE DREAM THAT YOU'RE FIGHTING
LEAVE ME NOW FOR EVERMORE

SONG OF RAIN

I WILL SING A SONG OF RAIN
LOOKS LIKE SILVER SPLINTERS
I WILL SAVE EACH LITTLE DRIP
FOR COUNTING UP THE WINTERS

I MAY LOOK KIND OF STRANGE
STROLLING IN THE WATER
WHAT IS RAIN, IS RAIN, IS RAIN
TO AN OTTER'S DAUGHTER?

LOOKS AS THOUGH THE RAIN HAS STOPPED
SAY "HI!" TO THE DRIZZLE
SENDING DOWN EACH LITTLE DROP
LANDING WITH A SIZZLE

WAY UP HIGH ON A MOUNTAIN TOP
THERE'S A GIRL WHO MAKES IT RAIN
THERE'S A BOY WHO MAKES IT STOP
THEY SIT AROUND AND ALWAYS COMPLAIN
HE WILL STOP THE RAIN FOR HER
SO SHE CAN START IT UP AGAIN
THEY SPREAD THE RAINBOW ON THE FLOOR
SHE WILL CAUSE THE RAIN TO START
SO HE CAN MAKE IT STOP ONCE MORE

THIS MORNING

THIS MORNING I LOOKED OUT YOUR WINDOW
THEN I WALKED OUT OF YOUR DOOR
I HAD A FEELING OF MAGIC
SOMETHING THAT I'VE FELT BEFORE

THE RAIN WAS WARBLING TO THE BIRDS
THE BIRDS HELD HANDS TO THE BLOSSOMS

I BECAME ME AGAIN
AND AGAIN BECAME AWESOME
  OH, I'M SO JOYFUL FOR WHAT WE SEE
  OH, I JUST LOVE TO BE FREE!

TIME

TIME, IT IS OUTSPOKEN
UNBROKEN LIKE A FAWN
AND THE MOON IS WEARY
DREARY WITH THE DAWN

SUN WAITS AT YOUR WINDOW
YOUR EYES FOLD TO YOUR PILLOW
THE DEW, IT IS A FROSTING
MOON BECOMES A WILLOW

WAKEN TO THE MORNING
YOUR HAND IT IS A THREAD
WIND SHAKES THE NIGHTTIME
FROM IT'S LIGHTENED HEAD

TO BYRON

YOU ASK YOURSELF "WHAT MISTAKE WAS MADE?"
"HAVEN'T I BEEN HERE BEFORE?"
YOU FIND YOURSELF TASTING DELIGHTS OF LOVE
SOMEHOW ALWAYS WANTING MORE

I CAN SEE YOUR FACE AND THE ONE YOU LOVE
A TRUTH THAT WILL ALWAYS EXIST
YOU'VE BROKEN EACH OTHER'S SOULS A THOUSAND TIMES
SOMEHOW YOU CANNOT RESIST

I CAN FEEL THE HURTING FROM YOUR EYES
I CAN HEAR YOUR CHOKING HEART
WHY IS IT JUST AS HARD TO BE
TOGETHER AS TO BE APART?

AND YOU ASK ME WHY DO I WRITE THIS SONG
AS I SIT HERE WAITING, WONDERING, FOR YOU
AND I ASK WHY AM I HERE AT ALL
I WONDER WHAT SHALL I DO?

WAGON / LET THE ROAD (LORD) BE YOUR FRIEND

CHANGING FROM YOUR RECKLESS WAYS
TAKES A STRENGTH THAT I CAN ONLY PRAISE
THAT VIOLENT FORCE YOU MUST NOW FIGHT
WILL NEVER BOW OUT OF SIGHT

AND WHEN FROM NO HUMAN YOU CAN GAIN
RESPITE FROM THIS DESPERATE PAIN
THE BROKEN SOUL NEEDS TIME TO MEND
SO LET THE ROAD (LORD) BE YOUR FRIEND

THE WAGON IS STRONG AND IT IS FRAIL
SOME MAKE THE JOURNEY, OTHERS FAIL

AND WHEN FROM NO HUMAN YOU CAN FIND
THE GRACE TO EASE YOUR TORTURED MIND
THE BROKEN SOUL NEEDS TIME TO MEND
SO LET THE ROAD (LORD) BE YOUR FRIEND

AND I KNOW YOU ARE FAR FROM YOUR HOME
BUT YOU'VE KNOWN THE ROAD (LORD) FROM LONG AGO

AND WHEN FROM NO HUMAN YOU CAN FIND
THE GRACE TO EASE YOUR TORTURED MIND
THE BROKEN SOUL NEEDS TIME TO MEND
SO LET THE ROAD (LORD) BE YOUR FRIEND

TIME IS BRUTAL AND LAYS WASTE
TO THOSE WHO ARE POWERLESS TO THE TASTE
THE WAGON IS STRONG AND IT IS FRAIL
SOME MAKE THE JOURNEY, OTHERS FAIL
I'M GRATEFUL FOR ANOTHER DAY
THE WAGON ROLLS ALONG THE PATHWAY!

AND WHEN FROM NO HUMAN YOU CAN GAIN
RESPITE FROM THIS DESPERATE PAIN
THE BROKEN SOUL NEEDS TIME TO MEND
SO LET THE ROAD (LORD) BE YOUR FRIEND

WHAT AM I THINKING?
ALL I CAN THINK OF ARE LOVE SONGS
ONE ENDS, THEN ONE MORE WILL START
THIS MUSIC THAT I'VE NEVER HEARD BEFORE
IS SUNG BY THE VOICE OF MY HEART

ALL I CAN FEEL NOW IS MAGIC
WITH RAINBOWS AND GENTLE SUNSHINE
I HAVE COME TO THE LAND WHERE DREAMS ARE MADE
FOR YOUR LIPS HAVE JUST BEEN TASTING MINE

YOU HAVE JOINED ME IN THE PRAIRIES
WE SHARE THE WONDER THAT FILLS THE SKY
I KNOW WE ARE TAKING THE SAME BREATH
I FEEL IT THE MOMENT WE SIGH!

ALL I CAN THINK OF ARE LOVE SONGS
PLEASE UNDERSTAND MY REPLIES
FOR THE ANSWER TO ANY MORE QUESTIONS
JUST LOOK ONCE AGAIN INTO MY EYES

YOU HAVE JOINED ME IN THE PRAIRIES
WE SHARE THE WONDER THAT FILLS THE SKY
I KNOW WE ARE TAKING THE SAME BREATH
I FEEL IT THE MOMENT WE SIGH!

ALL I CAN THINK OF ARE LOVE SONGS
PLEASE UNDERSTAND MY REPLIES
FOR THE ANSWER TO ANY MORE QUESTIONS
JUST LOOK ONCE AGAIN INTO MY EYES

YOU MAKE ME FEEL SO FINE

LOVE ME LIKE YOU DID YESTERDAY
I JUST LOVE YOU TO LOVE ME THE WAY
THE WAY YOU DO EVERYDAY,WHAT CAN I SAY!

I JUST LOVE TO HAVE YOU HOLD ME CLOSE
AND THE WAY THAT YOU KISS MY NOSE
THE WAY YOU FEEL, IT ALWAYS SHOWS
AND YOU LOVE ME WHEN I'M LOW
MAKES ME FEEL SO FINE, MAKES ME FEEL SO FINE

I JUST LOVE THE WAY YOU KISS ME
WHEN I'M GONE I KNOW YOU MISS ME
AND YOU MAKE ME FEEL SO FREE
SO HAPPY I CAN BE
MAKES ME FEEL SO FINE, MAKES ME FEEL SO FINE

YUPPIE LOVE

WHAT IS THERE TO REMEMBER
OF A FLAME THAT NEVER WANTED TO BURN
NO SPARKS TO START AND EMBER
OR ANXIOUS HEARTS THAT DANCE A SKIP, FLIP, OR CHURN?
THERE ARE NO MEMORIES TO REMIND US
OF THIS LOVE WE NEVER KNEW
OR MEMORIES TO BIND US WHEN WE FEEL SAD AS PEOPLE DO

I KEEP SEARCHING IN THE STARS FOR INSPIRATION BUT THEY ARE HIDING
THEN I TURN TOWARD THE MOON, SHE BECOMES BLANK AND NON-CONFIDING
I CALL TO THE RIVERS, AND THE MOUNTAINS TOO, THEY GENTLY SAY TO ME
"WHEN THERE IS NO LOVE TO REMEMBER THERE WILL BE NO MEMORIES"

WE'RE WASTING PRECIOUS TIME IN MEANINGLESS RELATIONSHIPS
IF A MEDIOCRE LIFE IS NOT WHAT YOU CHOOSE
JUST TURN TO NATURE, AND IF YOUR LOVE DOESN'T THRILL YOU SO
A BOREALIS! ALPENGLOW!
JUST SAY **NO!** TO YUPPIE LOVE!

THE PRAIRIE SAYS "STOP STRAINING
FIND SOMEONE OF WHOM YOU CAN'T HELP BUT SING
YOUR HEART WILL KICK AND START REFRAINING
MELODIES AND WORDS A'BUBB, BUBB–BUBBLING!
ALLITERATIONS TO HIS SMILE A MYRIORAMA OF HIS EYES
WHAT YOU'VE BEEN DREAMING ALL THE WHILE
IS NEVER FOUND IN COMPROMISE!"

I ASK THE BIRDS FOR FLOWERY PHRASES AND THEY START FLYING
TREES LEND NO IMPASSIONED WORDS FOR THEY SAY I WOULD BE LYING
I BEG THE SKY AND AS CLOUDS SWIM BY THEY GENTLY WAVE TO ME
"GO FIND YOURSELF A TRUE LOVE AND YOU'LL FIND THOSE MEMORIES"

WE'RE WASTING PRECIOUS TIME IN MEANINGLESS RELATIONSHIPS
IF A MEDIOCRE LIFE IS NOT WHAT YOU CHOOSE
JUST TURN TO NATURE, AND IF YOUR LOVE DOESN'T THRILL YOU SO
A BOREALIS! ALPENGLOW!
JUST SAY **NO!** TO YUPPIE LOVE!

YOUR PAST SAWS BACK AND FORTH AND BACK, ROUGHING AS IT FILES
YOUR RECORD SKIPS, BUT THE GROOVE EXQUISITE, FOR SOMEONE WHO SMILES!
Anatomy of a Melancoholic

ALTHOUGH NOT NUTRITIOUS FOR THE BIRDS, AT LEAST I COULD RECYCLE IT
I PUT IT OUTSIDE ON SOME ROCKS...I WAS TIRED OF LOOKING AT THE SHIT!
Montgomery Pie

POEMS OF FURY AND SHAME

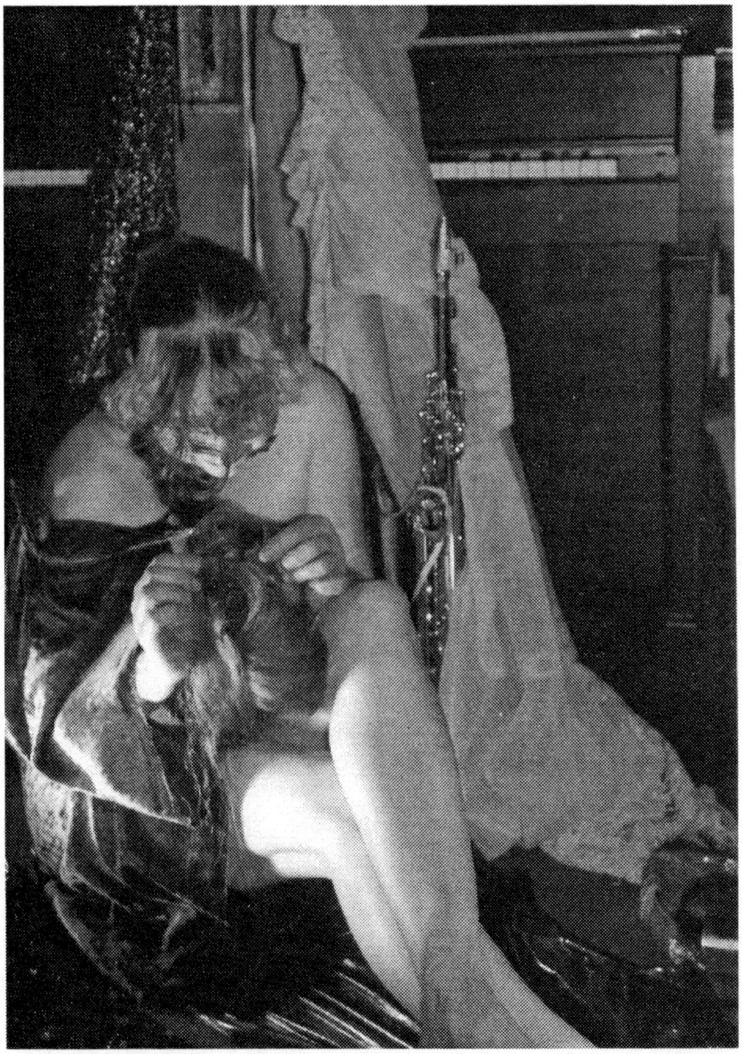

ANATOMY OF AN MELANCOHOLIC / THE SONG THAT NEVER

THE WAGON IS STRONG AND IT IS FRAIL, SOME MAKE THE JOURNEY, OTHERS FAIL

MAY 2005

WHEN I CAME TO YOU THAT NIGHT AFRAID SHOULD I HAVE NOT EXPRESSED MY NEED?
MY WORDS YOU SPEAR BEFORE THEY'RE MADE, ASK FOR THE PROPER PLACE TO BLEED
EACH SENTENCE RIPE TO TASTE IS STUNG, RETICENCE I MUST REHEARSE
FEELINGS ELSEWHERE SHALL BE HUNG WHERE THEY CANNOT INVITE A CURSE!

I, ANXIOUS TO READ HOW MY PEN PLAYS IN FORMS OF JOY THAT LAST
AM ROBBED OF UNBORN PHRASE, YOUR STERN REMAND "WE MOVE TOO FAST!"
WHAT INSIDE YOU DEEMS TO MAIM? THERE IS NO HUMOR IN THIS GAME
WHAT WRECKAGE YOU HAVE CRUMBLED THROUGH, YOU DRAG ME THROUGH THE SAME!

I HAD A DREAM–ALL HAD YOUR FACE–YOU POISED, THEN DREW YOUR MASK
IN TRIUMPH SHOWING OFF THE TRACKS OF UNHAPPINESS AT TASK!
WERE LIGHT TO DROWN GLOOM FROM BEHIND THOSE TRAGIC ORBS YOU STARE
WORDS THAT BEGGED TO SWIM COULD RISE ABOVE YOUR DREADFUL SNARE!

DECEMBER 2006

HOW BLUE THE BLUE RIDGE THAT I HAVE LOOKED TO WITH JOY
ONE YEAR PLUS ONE-HALF SINCE I MET THAT BOY
I WONDER HOW GLOOM CHOOSES ONE TO FASHION IN ITS STYLES
WHERE YOU ONCE? COULD YOU EVER BE SOMEONE WHO SMILES?

THROUGH OPTIMISM'S THICKENED MUTE MELODIES FAIL REFRAINS
HAPPY TUNES ARE STRANGLED ON OUR DREAR ROMANTIC SKEINS
YOUR PAST SAWS BACK AND FORTH AND BACK ROUGHING AS IT FILES
YOUR RECORD SKIPS, BUT THE GROOVE EXQUISITE, FOR SOMEONE WHO SMILES

FEBRUARY 2007

A TWINK AT YOUR MOUTH'S CORNER SHOW SMILES CAN MATERIALIZE!
A SUBTLE GLINT OF BRIGHTNESS SHOVES BEHIND YOUR BLUE-FULL EYES!
NOT THAT YOU'VE STOPPED TAKING DRINK AND PILLS FOR SADNESS CAUSED BY DRINK
GIANT TRUTH STARES FROM ALL DIMENSIONS AND DISOBEYS YOUR BLINK!

IN TRUTH THIS MELANCOHOLIC HAD NO RUINOUS PHYSIOLOGY OF BRAIN
EGREGIOUS WASTE OF HUMAN SPIRIT BLED FROM A **POISON'S** DRAIN
MY WORDS CONFINED TO NOTEBOOK NEEDED TIME TO SET THEM FREE
I AM **THE SONG THAT NEVER**, CONTENT AS POEM–SANS MEOLDY

BROKEN RECORD MENU FOR THE DAY

1st Course: do not get out of bed
your choice–no breakfast

Breakfast Special: Can't get out of bed over easy
Combination #1 Depression toast
Thoughts scrambled

Task #1: start with biological children feed on guilt 2 hours
(now it is 2:00 p.m.)
Go on to 1st ex-wife
Broken record–play for 20 minutes
Proceed to 2nd ex-wife
broken record play for 30 minutes
do some housework
current girl friend–guilt for having this relationship
add to broken record–play for 3 hours
feel fear of her leaving–
switch back to childhood beatings
switch back to God
switch back to whatever
I don't know anymore—just known you for a year.

CUPID

for once, you lost your vigilance
Cupid struck in certainty before you could turn around

you could have plucked his dainty spear from your toughened skin
you denied its mark and let it burrow deep within

it takes more than guts and bravery than to a dragon slay
to stand before the face of love and gladly give your heart away
instead of congratulating, making kin of your clever foe
you sneered "I have no time for playing!" and in anger turned to go!

DOPE-SNIFFING DOG

OH, HOW I WISH I HAD A DOPE-SNIFFING DOG
SO I COULD LIVE PEACEABLY
SO MANY COMINGS AND GOINGS I GAVE UP TRYING TO LOG
AND _____, IT'S ALL YOUR FAULT AS YOU SEE!

I KNOW THE POLICE DON'T HAVE SUCH AN ANIMAL TO LOAN
I GUESS THEY'RE TOO MUCH OF AN EXPENSE
BUT MAYBE I COULD BUY A DOG AND TRAIN IT AT HOME
I'D TEACH HIM TO BARK AT INCENSE

HE SHOULDN'T HAVE TROUBLE PICKING UP THE SCENT
AND HE'S SURE TO BECOME QUITE EXCITED
THEY'LL BE ABLE TO HEAR HIS BARK DOWN THE BASEMENT VENT
AS SOON AS THE INCENSE THEY'VE LIGHTED

I'D PUT HIM OUTSIDE AND WITH A FRIENDLY AIR
HE'D CASUALLY WHIFF OF TENANTS AND THEIR'S VISITOR'S CLOTHING
THEN HIS TAIL WOULD TURN STIFF AND HE'D BRISTLE HIS HAIR
AND GROWL WITH CONTEMPT, HATRED AND LOATHING

I'D LEAD HIM OUTSIDE IN FRONT OF #____ DOWN THE SIDES AND BEHIND
NO ONE WOULD KNOW HE WAS BLUFFING
TO THE TENANTS' FRONT DOORS, HE'D GROWL BY MY HAND SIGN
SURE TO SCARE THE GUILTY RIGHT OUT OF THEIR STUFFING!

BUT, I HAVE OTHER IDEAS TO CLEAN UP THE PLACE
I COULD RIG UP A FIFTEEN FOOT BANNER
"GET YOUR DOPE HERE" WOULD READ ACROSS #___'S FACE
SURE TO CAUSE VISITORS TO AVOID YOUR FINE MANOR

OR, IF ONLY I COULD BORROW A POLICE UNIFORM
NO, ____, MY MIND **NEVER** DOES STOP
HEY, I KNOW WHAT ELSE WOULD MAKE THE PLACE WARM
WHY DON'T I JUST DATE A COP?

AND LET ME TELL YOU ABOUT THE TENANTS
THAT INHABIT THIS BLESSED ABODE
I WOULD THINK IT WOULD MAKE YOU WANT TO DO PENANCE
TO LET THINGS OCCUR IN THIS MODE

THE YOUNG FATHER IN #1 THREW A GLASS GLOBE AT HIS GIRLFRIEND
WHILE THEIR INFANT LAY ON HER LAP
_____, I SAW THE MESS, BUT YOU CAN'T PRETEND
THAT THIS IS A COMMON MISHAP

HE WENT THROUGH A RADICAL PERSONALITY CHANGE
ONE MOMENT HE WAS NICE, THEN HE THREATENED TO KILL
THE MURDERS DOWN THE STREET–WAS **THAT** FELLOW DERANGED?
THINK ABOUT IT _____, DOES IT MAKE YOU ILL?

HOW WILL YOU DEAL WITH DEATH IF IT SHOULD COME
TO VISIT #___ PREMATURELY?
I FEEL LIKE A POOR PERSON STUCK IN A SLUM
BECAUSE OF NEIGHBORS THAT GO SQUIRRELY

I DO NOT EXCUSE YOU FROM THIS, ____, NO, NOT **ONE** FRACTION
FOR I THINK OF THIS AWAKE NIGHT AND DAY AND WHILE SLEEPING
YOU ARE GUILTY OF NEGLECT AND INACTION
AND NIGHTMARES ARE NOW IN MY DREAMS KEEPING

ASK MY NEIGHBOR NEXT DOOR LATELY WHAT **SHE'S** BEEN DREAMING
AND THIS HAS BEEN GOING ON FOR A YEAR
AND THE NOISE, THE CONSTANT NOISE **UPSTAIRS** AND COMPANY STREAMING
TO SEE YOUR LITTLE LAMB, YOUR CONVERTED DEAR

YES, SHE HAS CHANGED HER WAYS AND SWEARS THAT SHE WILL PRAY
NOTHING WORKS BETTER OR FASTER
THEN TURNING TO THE LORD IF RENT YOU CANNOT AFFORD
BUT WHO, OR **WHAT?...REALLY** IS HER MASTER?

HER BOY AND HIS PALS THINK THE STAIRS ARE A TRAMPOLINE
YOU SERVED HER LAST YEAR WITH A WARNING OF EVICTION
BUT SHE STILL LIVES HERE, SERENE IS THE SWEET LITTLE QUEEN
'CAUSE YOU ARE SNOW-JOBBED BY HER NEW CONVICTION

LET ME TELL YOU _____, ABOUT THE BICYCLES
THINGS YOU ALREADY KNOW
IN FAIR WEATHER, THROUGH SNOW AND BELOW ICICLES
THEY NEVER STOP, THEY NEVER SLOW

I HEAR THE WIND SWISH THROUGH THE SPOKES OF THEIR WHEELS
THEN IT STOPS AS THEY'RE LAIN SWIFTLY DOWN ON EARTH OR UPON SNOW
PORTENTS OF PURPOSE POWERED BY YOUTHFUL HEELS
I DRIFT BACK TO SLEEP—A NIGHTMARE TONIGHT?–MAYBE NO

WHEN I HEAR THAT SWISH PAST MY BEDROOM WINDOW AT NIGHT
IT CONJURES IMAGES OF SOME KIND OF WINGS
BUT IT HAS A SOUND THAT ISN'T QUITE RIGHT
OMINOUS OF SINISTER THINGS

I THINK OF PEOPLE WHO HAVE LOST CONTROL OF THEIR SOULS
A TOLL-TAKING OF SPIRITS SO YOUNG
SLAVES TO SUBSTANCES THAT HAUNT AND CONTROL
THIS LAMENT WITHIN #____'S WALLS IS SUNG!

YOU KNOW, _____, ABOUT THE BICYCLES, HOW THEY COME AND GO
AND ARE ABANDONED IN THE NEIGHBOR'S BACK YARD
BUT WHAT ARE THEY DOING, ____?, YOUR MIND IS NOT SLOW
NEIGHBORS AND I NEVER **DO** RELAX, WE MUST ALWAYS BE ON GUARD

_____, YOU DON'T THINK OF WHAT YOU SHOULD TAKE STOCK
(DID YOU OWN #_____, WHEN LAST IT WAS BUSTED?)
IN CASE A POLICE ACTION OCCURS ON THIS BLOCK
DO YOU REMEMBER, OR IS YOUR MEMORY RUSTED?

BUT ENOUGH OF MY FELLOW TENANTS, I DO NOT FEEL THAT THEY ARE BAD
I SAY HELLO TO SOME, AND EVEN CONVERSE
BUT YOU, ____, **YOU** ARE VERY SAD
YOU THE LANDLORD, _____, ARE THE CURSE!

YOUR NEIGHBORS TRIED TO BUY #___ SOME TIME AGO
BECAUSE OF PAST HAPPENINGS AND WHAT MIGHT OCCUR
YOUR SELLING PRICE TOLD THEM YOUR ANSWER WAS NO
HOW MUCH MORE SHOULD THEY AND I ENDURE?

_____, WHY IS THE WIRING NOT UP TO CODE?
WHEN YOU BOUGHT THE PLACE, THIS YOU MUST HAVE KNOWN
I'M TELLING YOU NOW SO IGNORANCE IS NO DEFENSE
THE TENANT IN #2 WON'T SQUAWK, HE'S BEHIND IN HIS RENTS

I GUESS HE FEELS HE DOESN'T HAVE A RIGHT TO SAFETY
ASK FORMER TENANT OF #1–SHE **KNOWS** ABOUT THE ELECTRICITY
AND ME, WELL, I'VE NOT CHECKED IT'S RELIANCE
I SCARCELY RUN MORE THAN ONE APPLIANCE

LET'S TALK ABOUT LAST NIGHT WHEN #2'S STOVE WENT **BOOM!**
IT WOKE UP THE BABY IN THE NEXT ROOM
I HEARD IT AND I LIVE NEXT DOOR
IT STARTLED ME, BUT I CHOSE TO IGNORE

THE TENANTS SCREAMED, BUT I NEVER THOUGHT TO GIVE AID
THE NOISE STOPPED SO I TOLD MYSELF TO NOT BE AFRAID
I THINK IT'S OKAY TO BUY APPLIANCES THAT ARE DISCARDED
BUT _____, YOU ARE SO **COLD-HEARTED!**

#2'S REFRIGERATOR FOR MONTHS HAS BEEN LEAKING
YOU KNOW ABOUT WHAT I AM SPEAKING!
AND THEIR CEILING IS STILL FALLING APART
BUT THEY'RE BEHIND IN THEIR RENT, SAY, ____, YOU'RE PRETTY SMART!

ASK FORMER TENANT #1 ABOUT THE BREAKERS, AND #2 THE WALL SOCKET
HE'D COMPLAIN IF HE HAD MONEY IN HIS POCKET
AND WHY DID MPC TURN OFF THE WATER HEATER IN JANUARY?
WHEN I SMELLED GAS IN MY APARTMENT, IT GOT RATHER SCAREY

I HAD THE CATS READY FOR EVACUATING
AND AIRED OUT THE PLACE WHILE FOR MPC I WAS WAITING
THE VERDICT—DANGERS FROM CARBON MONOXIDE, FIRE AND EXPLOSION
ILLEGAL VENTING, STRESSED PIPES AND EROSION

YOU WERE UNABLE TO TALK MPC INTO TURNING IT BACK ON
SO WE COULD NOT HAVE HOT WATER BECAUSE YOU WERE GONE
AND UNABLE IT FIX IT YOURSELF--TO SAVE MONEY
IT COST YOU SIX HUNDRED BUCKS! AND TO YOU THAT AIN'T FUNNY!

WHEN I TRIED TO GET YOU BY PHONE YOU REFUSED MY COLLECT CALL
IT WOULD GO ON TO YOUR DAUGHTER'S BILL, AND THAT ISN'T ALL
I CALLED YOU IN ______, IT COULD HAVE BEEN AN EMERGENCY
BUT THE COST OF A COLLECT CALL! GOODNESS SAKES—POOR _____!

YOU WOULDN'T SPRING FOR REPAIRS UNTIL MONDAY, BUT THAT'S PAR
FOR SOMEONE AS FRANTIC ABOUT MONEY AS YOU ARE
THE REPAIRMAN "COULDN'T BELIEVE..."–GUESSED IT WAS "OWNER INSTALLED"
THE WATER HEATER, THE COST,...I BET YOU BAWLED!

AND THIS IS THE REASON, ____, YOU DON'T HAVE ANY SENSE
YOU DON'T CARE WHO LIVES IN #___ YOU DON'T CARE WHO RENTS
DO YOU GET WEAK ____, WHEN YOU THINK OF CASH?
DO YOU LIKE TO SPEND IT OR JUST ADD TO YOUR STASH?

BUT REALLY, ____, YOU LOSE MORE BY THE TENANTS YOU KEEP
YOU GO AHEAD AND RENT TO ANY TYPE OF CREEP
BUT PERHAPS IT'S THE GAMBLE THAT YOU LIKE, AND WHAT'S AT STAKE
MAYBE YOU'RE HOOKED ON THE FEAR OF WHAT YOU **WON'T** MAKE!

FOR INSTANCE, FROM I HEAR YOU STAND TO LOSE
FIFTEEN HUNDRED BUCKS IF EVICTING IS WHAT YOU CHOOSE
NOW, ISN'T THAT A FINE REASON TO LET THE TENANTS REMAIN
LOOK AT ALL THE EXTRA MONEY YOU MAY NOT GAIN!

AND **HERE** IS WHERE I HIT BELOW THE BELT
GET READY, ____, THINK OF HOW FOR A YEAR **I'VE** FELT!
YOU'VE COMPLAINED ABOUT MONEY GOING TO FUNERAL AND CHURCH
TRY TO THINK OF WHAT'S KEEPING YOU ON SUCH A PERCH!

THAT YOU CAN EXPECT THE POLICE AND NEIGHBORS TO HELP YOU WITH THIS!
I WON'T ____, YOU ARE SORELY REMISS!
BUT I'LL TELL YOU WHAT YOU MUST DO
BETTER CHANGE THAT **GREED** THAT TAKES HOLD OF YOU!

I FOUND A NAME FOR WHAT AILS **YOU** AND YOU GOT IT BAD, ____,
YOU WON'T FIND IT IN ANY BUT **MY** DICTIONARY

"HYPERLACKOFTENDERPHOBICLANDLORTENANTITIS"

ALSO KNOWN AS

"INEEDMONEYSOIDON'TGIVEAHOOTWHOOCCUPIESIT"

NEXT TIME GREED BECOMES YOUR MASTER

RUN OUT THE DOOR ____, GO FIND YOUR PASTOR!

DRAGON

YOU MADE FRIENDS WITH THE DRAGON WHO WAS OUT TO KILL OUR LOVE
THEN ASKED ME TO FORGIVE YOUR ALLEGIANCE!

WHILE YOU BEDDED DOWN WITH THE BEAST
WHO IN FEMALE GARB
YOU MINIMIZED THE BARB
AND POURED YOUR LOVE OVER MY GRIEVANCE

NO LONGER SHALL YOU TOUCH MY HAND
NOR CATCH AFFECTION IN MY EYES
A BETRAYAL YOU'VE NO ACKNOWLEDGMENT OF SURRENDER
YOU WHINE LIKE A BRAT!
AND EXPECT THAT A PRECIOUS THING AS LOVE
IS READY TO BE AT YOUR WILL–SAVED–GROW TENDER

AFTER YOU HAVE DEFILED A HEART YOU DID NOT OWN

I GAVE YOU THE KNOWLEDGE TO FIGHT THE BEAST
AND YOU AGREED TO THE BATTLE PLAN
THEN GAVE IN TO A WEAK MAN'S ABYSS OF VALOR
AND BECAME WHAT YOU REALLY ARE, AND YOU ARE VAIN

WHILE THE DRAGON TORE DOWN WITH PREMEDITATED FEMININE DEFTNESS
A SHALLOW DEFENSELESS LOVE
AND THE DRAGON BEGGED YOU NOT TO CAUSE HER PAIN
HER PAIN WAS YOUR DUTY TO CODDLE
FOR SHE HAD MORE EMINENCE THAN THE NEW LOVE YOU PROFESSED

SO YOU SLEPT WITH THE DRAGON, IF ONLY FOR COMFORT
BUT FOR WHOM?

GO AWAY FROM MY DOOR!
ACCEPT YOUR CHOICE
YOU SAY THERE IS NO BLACK AND WHITE

THERE IS GOOD AND EVIL!
THERE IS DESPERATION!
THERE IS BETRAYAL!
THERE IS SELFISHNESS AND VANITY!
THERE IS INDECENCY AND RECKLESSNESS!
THERE IS CRUELTY!

GO AWAY FROM MY DOOR!
YOU MADE A CHOICE
THERE NEVER **WAS** A SPECIAL LOVE THAT YOU FINALLY FOUND
MY DOOR IS BANISHED UNDER BARREN GROUND!

FIRST YEAR ANNIVERSARY

the hairs on your mustache magnified the
pore from which the hair comes out of the
folds around your mouth wrapping around
my mind
let me enjoy this visit
let me taste and smell everything–let
me not miss a thing
I am gone somewhere
in your kiss
I am enfolded somewhere
not lost here--here
enjoying the warmth–being taken in
part of that moustache with each
magnified hair
part of that mouth is mine
and when we pause–I am back on
the riverbank–a chilly September
afternoon–a little wind but not really
chilly because we are on a blanket–two
blankets–in the grasses–the Autumn-colored
grasses and the river but we are snuggled

on the earth–cuddling one another–we
are warm and pause and then roll
around in rapture–giggle–drink in
each other's eyes–focus on this one–that
one seeing a wrinkle where the eye was then
another eye–focusing in and out like a child
but all this is the face with the eye
and the wrinkle where a nose might be
and another eye when focusing loses the
other eye and then coming up for air
another squeeze--giggle--a feast of
flesh–warm–soft flesh underneath the
clothing–watching you taste my flesh–watching
you watch me while you are tasting me
the aroma of my strategically placed scented
oils–carefully placed so that if you were to
get close to me you would be enveloped in
the scents I hoped would entice you to enjoy me
do you know what prose is? Do I...?
I will read this to you so you
will know how it is to be read
I will read you back the day we spent
together–lovers–but not lovers–
my finding joy in teasing you–taking enough
of you for myself–and not giving you
too much
I slapped you today on your face with an
artful hand–slightly–but with reprimand
you were naughty–and went through the door
before me–I pulled you back–and slapped you
like I had been dreaming of so–and you
deserved it–but your face did not turn
red but you got the message–I felt
proud like it was so controlled–thought of–
premeditated–and delivered without pain–
without force–but having precision–
I could never have practiced for years and done so well...

IF I WERE A BITCH

if I were a bitch
I'd be very rich
men would simply adore me
instead, I am nice
and have no price
so men never do anything for me

if I were a bitch
I'd have twelve men on a hitch
and all of them at my disposal
a day would not pass
when they'd not give the world for my ass
and be on their knees in proposal!

I'd be coy and mysterious
and they'd all be serious
I'd have the world on a string!
my life would be laughter
I'd have what they're after
and a warehouse of presents they'd bring

I'd have diamonds and gold
beaus, medium, young and old
of all physical descriptions
I'd see how I feel
then choose from my wheel
of fortune, for whom would fill my prescription

on a day that is grey
I'd pick one to play
games that go well with hot cocoa
on a day that is gloomy
I'd have another sing to me
ballads in voce sotto

On a day that is sunny
I'd take one who is funny
we'd take off for a week in his plane
we'd see Rome and Tennessee
Africa and Hawaii
Timbuktu, The Casbah and Spain

On a day that is raining
I'd start complaining
so I'd be promised a car.
since I had a BMW
Rolls, Bentley, and Cord too
I'd settle on a pink Jaguar

my men would be charming,
handsome and disarming
full of sincere trust and devotion
they'd be full or passion and lust
and all that a man must
have to arouse my emotion!

but where are these men?
I search over and again
and find not one who suits my taste
with all my running around
I'd think at least **one** I'd have found
but my activities have gone to waste!

I have no coat of armor
rich man or poor farmer
who gives a damn! I try them all
if I find them appealing
and they awaken some feeling
why then, on earth, should I stall!

a man who has many lovers
and spends much time under covers
is not often neglected
a woman who does the same
gets a bad name
and is always rejected

so, I pay for my passion
while a bitch would cash in
with a tact that is much admired
for the piles of wealth
gained by cunning and stealth
lying on her back has acquired

so, I doubt that I'll ever
become smart or clever
and I sit here with a lonely heart
while I could be progressing
instead of depressing
by selling my ass as an art!

LAST REQUEST

I HEAR YOU BELCHING OUTSIDE AT THE BARBEQUE GRILL
I WANT YOU TO LEAVE, BUT INSTEAD I SIT STILL
WHILE YOU'RE PLAYING WITH HAMBURGERS AND SWAYING ON YOUR FEET
YOU'RE TALKING ABOUT DRIVING SOMEWHERE TO EAT!

WITH SNUFF STUFFED IN YOUR CHEEK AND A BEER IN YOUR HAND
HOW FAR WILL YOU PASS FIFTY-ONE BEFORE YOU UNDERSTAND?
YOU NEED TO PRACTICE HOW TO ENJOY BEING ALONE
IF GOD WERE AT THE BAR WITH YOU, **HE'D** SEND YOU HOME!

LEARN COMFORT WITHIN YOURSELF AND IF THAT
IS TOO SCARY TRY THE COMPANIONSHIP OF A CAT
YOU WON'T HAVE A WOMAN, YOU WANT RESPECT FROM YOUR KIDS
SURE, A LONELY DEVOTED DRUNK DADDY ON THE SKIDS!

WITH TWO DUI'S TO YOUR NAME
YOU DON'T HAVE A PROBLEM, YOU CLAIM
YOU'RE A RANCHER, FIT WITH THE PERSONALITY
FOR BLAMING, COMPLAINING, EVADING REALITY!

OH, YOU MAY HAVE A TOUGH GUT, YOU MAY NEVER GET ILL
BUT YOUR SPIRIT IS DYING, SO IS YOUR WILL
AND YOUR WORST FEAR IS TO END UP LIKE YOUR UNCLE, JOE
OLD AND DECREPIT, ALONE AND SLOW!

WHAT'S HAPPENING, MY FRIEND? WHY–YOU ARE IN HELL!
AN ALCOHOL–BAR PRISON, YOUR MIND IS YOUR CELL
YOUR LIFE: DRINK–KIDS–RANCH–PARTY AND DANCE
NO TIME LEFT FOR A SORRY ATTEMPT AT ROMANCE!

SO, IF THE WORD "CHANGE" FILLS YOU WITH ALARM
TRY THE WORDS "IMPROVING WITH AGE" AND "DEVELOPING CHARM"
TELL YOUR DRINKING BUDDIES THAT YOU "...HAVE MATURED"
IF THEY DON'T LIKE YOU SOBER–FLIP THEM THE BIRD!

AND TELL THAT ASSHOLE BARTENDER WHO SERVED YOU AT THE BAR
HE SHOULD HAVE DRIVEN YOU HOME, TAKEN THE KEYS TO YOUR CAR!
I KNEW YOU WERE A LUSH, BUT THANKS FOR THE SHOW!
LOOK IN THE MIRROR AND GREET YOUR UNCLE JOE!

SO, IF THE MERE THOUGHT OF "CHANGING" FILLS YOU WITH ALARM
TRY, "IMPROVING WITH AGE" AND "DEVELOPING CHARM"
TELL ANY ASSHOLE WHO PROTESTS THAT YOU "HAVE MATURED"
HE CAN STAY IN HELL IF **HE** WANTS TO, THEN FLIP HIM THE BIRD!

LOVE IS A LIVING THING

MY HAND PLAYED TRICKS ON PAPER WITH A HURT AND ANGRY PEN
IT STARTED TO WRITE AWAY OUR LOVE THEN TRIED TO WRITE IT BACK AGAIN
"LOVE IS A LIVING THING" IT WROTE ON EACH PAGE THAT WAS NEW
WAS I NOT SUPPOSED TO RETURN TO YOU?

THESE FIVE WORDS JOSTLED IN MY MIND AND DENIED OUR LOVE WAS GONE
THEY FORCED MY HAND AND STOLE INK AND PAPER THEY LIVE ON
YOUR EYES REACHED IN TO FLOOD MY HEART AND HOPE AND DARING FANNED
YOUR KISS EXPLAINED THE MESSAGE FROM MY HAND

YOUR EYES SHOW "LOVE IS A LIVING THING" I READ THEIR NAKEDNESS
THE MAN, THE BABE, THE CHILD THEY ALL PLEAD FOR MY CARESS
LOOK AGAIN AT ME–LIKE THAT! YOU'LL SEE MY SOUL,TOO, IS BARE
YOU ARE SUPPOSED TO HELP ME FIND SOMETHING SOMEWHERE!

"LOVE IS A LIVING THING THAT BEGS TO HAVE A CHANCE"
LOGIC VANISHES WHEN THE HEART ENTERS THE GALAXY, ROMANCE
TO FIND HOME BEYOND THE STARS A WORDLESS REALITY
AND LOVE'S GREATEST CHARM IS ITS MYSTERY

"LOVE IS A LIVING THING THAT SUFFERS WHEN IT DIES"
I STOP THE PAIN BY LOOKING THROUGH A DIFFERENT SET OF EYES
THE SAME DEAR YOU, A DIFFERENT VIEW AND ME AT DIFFERENT RANGE
BUT MY SPIRIT WILL NEVER HONOR SUCH A CHANGE

I CHANGED BECAUSE I THOUGHT MY WORDS ASKED SOMETHING DEAR OF ME
I AM SAD BECAUSE YOU DID NOT TEND TO OUR LOVE CAREFULLY
HOW FRUITLESS HAS THIS ATTEMPT TO IN LOVE'S FAVOR SWING
A HAPPY COURSE WHEN I'VE NOT THE CHOICE TO SAVE "LOVE, A LIVING THING"

MONTGOMERY PIE (SHAME PIE)

"SOMETHING YOU'VE NEVER HAD BEFORE"
A HARLEY T-SHIRT? A BIKER MAMA'S LEATHER GARMENT?
SOME SILVER MOTORCYCLE MEDALLION?

HE WAS STINGY WITH HIS TIME
I WAS UNSURE, ALMOST CERTAIN, ALTHOUGH UNABLE TO ADMIT..WITH MONEY ALSO
SUCH AN OPTIMIST AM I!
WITH GIDDY HOPE I WAITED FOR THE CHRISTMAS PRESENT

NOW, NOT ALL HORROR IS GORY
IT 'AINT WORTH MAKING THIS A LONG STORY

WAS THIS NEW LOVE ABOUT TO DIE?
WHEN BEARING THE CHRISTMAS GIFT OF...A PIE!

NOT QUITE A BACHELOR, IS SOMEONE A FOOL?
DID I GIVE HIM A KISS?..I DO NOT REMEMBER
BUT I WAITED UNTIL LATER DATE IN DECEMBER

PERHAPS IT WAS THE NEXT DAY WHEN I MADE UP MY MIND
NOT TO TOSS THE PIE BUT TO USE IT IN A CREATIVE KIND

IT TOLD HIM IT WAS "DELICIOUS" AS I RECALL
A REAL WOUND TO MY FEMININE ESTEEM
CAN WE EVEN SUSPECT WHAT ANOTHER SOUL MAY DREAM?
WHAT KIND OF CONSCIOUSNESS DWELLS IN THEIR BODIES?
THOSE BLUE EYES TELL NOTHING
AND I HAVE NO SAY IN WHAT HE IS FEELING

I AM ON MY OWN—I ANALYZED THE TASTE OF THAT PIE
FOR SEVERAL DAYS I TRIED TO EXTRACT SOME UNIQUE FLAVORS
HOPING FOR ONE...**PLEASE**... SMALL TINY HINT OF HEAVEN
BUT IT WAS JUST CRUMBLY CRUST, SUGARY, HAD A SLIGHT TASTE OF LEMON!

BUT IT WAS LIKE THREE LAYERS, THE CRUST THE MOIST DENSE LEMONY PART
AND SUGARY CRUMBLES ON TOP
I KEPT TASTING BUT WITH NO EXCITEMENT TO APPEASE OR
DELIGHT SO I PUT THE REMAINS IN THE FREEZER

NOT THAT **THAT** WOULD TRANSFORM IT INTO PLEASURE
BUT THIS ROMANTIC CHRISTMAS PRESENT WOULD TEACH ME A LESSON
AND I USED IT AS A TOOL TO PUNISH MY HOPEFUL HEART

HE KNEW I HAD NEVER HAD MONTGOMERY PIE BEFORE
BECAUSE HE HAD ASKED ME
WE COULD HAVE FOUND A WAY TO SPEND SOME CHRISTMAS TIME TOGETHER
THE DESIRE WAS NOT THERE ON HIS PART

SO WHEN THE HOLIDAY WAS OVER
I STILL HAD THE REMAINS OF THE PIE IN MY FREEZER
DID I GAIN INSIGHT EACH TIME I SAW IT THERE...**NO!**

A STING OF LONELINESS AND FUTILITY...YES!...HUMILITY!
HUMOR?...NOT YET

IT NEVER GOT BETTER IN ITS PLASTIC CONTAINER
IT LOOKED FROSTED OVER...I KNEW I SHOULD NO LONGER CLING
TO THE HOPES OF MAKING SOMETHING OUT OF THIS UGLY THING

ALTHOUGH NOT NUTRITIOUS FOR THE BIRDS, AT LEAST I COULD RECYCLE IT
I PUT IT OUTSIDE ON SOME ROCKS...I WAS TIRED OF LOOKING AT THE SHIT!

I TOOK PICTURES TRYING TO MAKE AESTHETICISM OF SUNLIGHT
BOUNCING OFF THE PEAKS OF THE CRUMBLES THROUGH THE BLAND LEMON FILLING
AND BORING CRUST

YOU FINALLY FOUND TIME TO SEE ME, THOUGH I WOULD HAVE LOVED TO SEE THOSE
FINE BLUE EYES AND YOUR COOKING WOULD HAVE BEEN A REAL TREAT
I HAD TO TELL YOU WAS TOO WOUNDED AFTER THE CHRISTMAS GIFT FROM A
SWEETHEART OF SOMETHING TO EAT!!!

SILENCED HURT

If we choose not to discuss this matter
it will make a little wound
for a spot is now made tender there
and if another hurt is done
and we are not aware

a wound will start because the tender spot
had to yield to pain
and if not healed or soothed by caring
it can grow again

until another hurtful word or act
will build upon this sore
all this because the first matter not resolved
because we chose to ignore

a woman's heart will suffer long
in mute compliancy
the silence stings as salt to wounds
and spears all decency

and as time goes on this angry sore
spreads devastating pain
the only choice–to cut the heart--
is this what you choose to gain?

STOLEN KISSES

I SEE THAT BULGE BENEATH YOUR LIP
WHERE YOU'VE STUFFED THAT GRIMY DRIP
WHEN BLACK GOO ON YOUR MOUTH OR CHIN DOES STICK
I'M CONVINCED THAT YOU MUST BE PART HICK!

YOU LEAVE A SLIME ON MY FACE
AND A SHARP TOBACCO TRACE
SOMETIMES I WIPE IT OFF WHEN YOUR HEAD IS TURNED
I FEEL LIKE MY LIPS HAVE JUST BEEN BURNED!

I AM TRULY GRATEFUL YOU ARE MY FRIEND
BUT FOR THIS, A WOMAN WAS NOT MEANT TO BEND
I'VE FAILED WHERE I VOWED TO NOT BE REMISS
AND SURRENDERED MY REVERENCE OF THE KISS!

YES, IT IS TRUE, YOUR HABIT WENT RIGHT BY ME
I JUST THOUGHT YOUR KISSES WERE NORMALLY SLIMY
AND YOU ARE SPECIAL, SO I'VE TRIED MY BEST
TO KNOW YOU, THOUGH YOU FAILED THE KISSING TEST

VOLUMES OF LITERATURE WILL PROVE
A KISS CAN BE THE MOST IMPORTANT MOVE
WITH A WOMAN WHO CAN ACHIEVE THE PUREST BLISS
RESULTING FROM A SINGLE KISS

YOU'VE LEARNED TO SWALLOW INSTEAD OF SPIT
THUS, PROVING THE HYGIENE OF YOUR HABIT
SPITTLE IS SELDOM SEEN ON YOUR CHIN
BUT SNUS STICKS IN YOUR TEETH AND SHOWS WHEN YOU GRIN

IT MAKES YOUR CHIN LOOK AS IF IT IS DEFORMED
BUT AT LEAST MY LIPS ARE FOREWARNED
AND I CAN WITHDRAW WITH A FRIENDLY PECK
ALTHOUGH AGAINST MY NATURE, I DECLINE TO NECK

YOU BELIEVE THAT SNUFF IS MADE OR HARMLESS BLACK CRUMBS
YOU'VE EVEN DISPLAYED YOUR RECEDING GUMS
TO SHOW THAT AFTER ALL THESE YEARS YOU DON'T HAVE LEUKOPLAKIA YET
AND TONGUE CANCER IS FOR SOMEONE ELSE TO GET!

YEAH, A MAN OWES IT TO HIMSELF TO HAVE AT LEAST **ONE** PITFALL
YEP!, HE'S PROUD TO ADMIT HE'S HUMAN AFTER ALL!
THERE'S A CERTAIN COMRADERY IN BEING A SLAVE
A MAN'S DUTY IS TO SATISFY HIS RIGHT TO CRAVE!

YOU TELL ME ONE BRAND EVEN CONTAINS GROUND-UP GLASS
SO MORE SWIFTLY THROUGH THE BLOODSTREAM IT WILL PASS
GEE, I WONDER! AM I SUPPOSED TO BE IMPRESSED!
THIS FINE SELLING POINT I WOULD NEVER HAVE GUESSED!

WELL, I'VE LEARNED TO RETREAT AFTER A QUICK SMOOCH
TOBACCO SLAVER IS LIKE THE LICK OF A POOCH
A FACET OF ROMANCE ENDS DUE TO THIS
AS I DISCOVER THE MEANING TO "STEALING A KISS"!

STUPID DRUNKEN FACE

How I loathe your stupid drunken face!
If you die before me–will it ever erase?
I dream about your stupid drunken face
and wake up sad–but it's not only a dream

How I hate your stupid drunken face!
Each time I see it, it takes weeks to erase
weekends spoiled–leisure time lost
how many days have you stolen with

your stupid drunken face?
What did **I** do in life?
Is this part of your punishment?
to punish me with you your stupid drunken face?
Your two ex-wives–did they like your
stupid drunken face?

Next time your face is drunken stupid
don't let me see your stupid drunken face!
Don't sleep with me and don't talk
to me–don't let me see you the next
morning!

How often will this happen?
        Once a month?
        Once a month on a weekend
        and during leisure time?

Let me know so I can get **away**
from that stupid drunken face!
it stays in my mind and when
people ask me how I am, I have
to tell them–"lousy"–I saw that
stupid drunken face again!

TEARS

FOR THOSE WHO DO NOT OFFER SPRING
THEIR TEARS TO SPREAD AS BLOSSOMS FALL
THE KEPT TEARS WILL STING
AT SUMMER'S CALL

TEARS WILL CONDENSE SUMMER'S RAYS
AND THIRST DEARLY FOR A COOLING BREEZE
NO NEW LOVE'S KISS WILL LIFT THE HAZE
OF TEARS GUARDED THROUGH THE SULTRY EVES

FALL WILL THINK YOUR TEARS ARE FUN
AND WHIP THEM FROM YOU DEMANDING MORE
GATHERING ON A WILD RUN
TO FLING THEM BACK 'TIL YOUR EYES ARE SORE!

KEEP YOUR TEARS THROUGH WINTER'S FROST!
BLEAK DAYS AND NIGHTS WILL NEVER END
AND WHEN YOU HAVE BECOME BEYOND LOST
TEARS WILL BE YOUR ONLY FRIEND!

THE TWELVE BEERS OF FISHMUST / HAPPY FATHER'S DAY!

The 1st beer in the truck is 'cause you're going fishing
The 2nd because the 1st one tasted good
The 3rd for preparation for your launch into the water
The 4th through 6th in hopes bass bite the way they should
The 7th cause you started thinking about the first wife
and your two kids that you did wrong
You lament not her, but the for the second wife who left **you**
The 8th beer like clockwork, comes along

The 9th is to help you with your daughter
whose visitation will end when she's eighteen
Then the 10th–and isn't it great to be out fishing!
Perhaps a nap with cap, forget the sun screen!

The 11th, 12th, now--what will be your story?
And don't forget to stash the bottles before you leave
the boat is in the garage safely, you--in glory
remember--up the stairs and do not slur or weave

I made sure when you returned I would be sleeping
your entry noiseless! To not disturb, your fondest hope
angels must assisted you in creeping
but they deserted you in handling of soap!

I woke to the cake escaping during your shower
it was like a noisy game of cat and mouse
I lie still to numb a spirit that is sour
will Sleep erase unhappy nights inside this house?

WAS IT LOVE?

Was it Love that flitted around our might
a gift we lost, transient, bright
and sharp-witted to endear by candlelight?

Was it Love that tottered and then fell in tiny sharp strings
that whipped away in April winds
and darted in and out to place its stings
on some poor heart foolishly waiting for some things?

Was it Love you traded carelessly
that for a moment let you view?
And did it give the choice to receive or betray
promising chances for another day?

WILD MEAT

"..once you've had a taste..." What **was** it she meant with that sly smile when I had just discovered and raved about wild game?—Ruby knew I liked men.

"I'd **kill** for venison" was my reply to my boss's offer of deer meat which I told him I would rent freezer space to accommodate, he was generous, I was rich again.

Mr. Tequila

"Where's my meat?"
"When we get back from dinner." was his reply.

Off went his clothes for a bathrobe
the fire was not appealing to me
and I did not want to start this nothingness again

The dog was just an extra, not a house pet
the guinea pig was on the cold laundry floor and I advocated
for its placement in a sunny social spot

the margaritas were o.k. but I left feeling shallow
and he forgot to give me my wild game

next time someone mentioned deer bologna I said
"You really don't want to promise me **that** if you are going to forget!"
He did not forget my deer bologna
but I will never forgive Mr. Tequila for not giving me
the promised wild meat

WINDOWS TO YOUR SOUL

The leaden windows to your soul are unseeing
and retreat somewhere, perhaps unknown to you
where comes your voice that has stormed my being
and pulls me in and out and over, around and through?

Panic warned, but Pain's journey was my decision
and then a spell had begun to spread
though never wrong, I questioned Instinct's derision
then Possible refused to trade its place with Dread

As I choose to reside in Hope's dominion
perhaps I'll never have the love of my desired kind
but Reality is a farce, and its opinion
does not rule in this girlish mind!

and the spring without you
sheds cherry blossom tears that
bruise by the warm wind
Springtime Magnolia Collection 11

it scurried like rabbits
flurried the white block ink race
and buried forever itself
of obsidian spread
in ink brink day
Springtime Magnolia Collection 15

POEMS OF SPRINGTIME MAGNOLIA COLLECTION

1

I have in my life collected
a set of works undirected
feelings that are uncontained
incomplete and unrestrained
there are times when I
have left my being...
to confirm that I was
seeing

I know no risk, no
price, no fall
I know love
and that is all...

2

I shall descend to the
depth and un-alight
the night aloft
so softly I submerge
I know a sea of motionless
and I, regal... lower...mellow, accept
the arm that was
and is always expecting
my calmity, and subsiding
confiding to
my very stalk of nature
greets me, swing to me
myself and bring me back to
where I shall ascend and
un-alight the night aloft so softly
I...

3 nome

as clearing your self
of cluttering objects, so that
inside you may rest nondistracted
also should you prepare
for living in a gentle way
to stretch the mind in
accepting the wideness of an ocean
and, again belong

4

I believe that I am through
with centering my problems
around you
I now admit
and remember the voice
all during my life cries out,
he that is weighted by
the cross,
raises that of his own choice
and must know that to stumble and to fall
is not to be questioned
if he bear the cross at all...

5

there doesn't seem to be
a way out of here
and each day I try to be better
but the time isn't coming near

be it now that I am able
or may it be tomorrow
that I sing a portrait
paint my words tamed by sorrow

and now I now you are lost
only because you wish to be
and forever is a long time
to try to forget about me

and I love you
but how can it mean a thing
because of all these years
you tried to teach me how not to sing

my mind is awaiting
and my spirit is broken
I need a careful wisdom
to survive these words that I have spoken

6

you sidled a pathway into
my acknowledgment, unthirsted...
a warm wind smiling
on my forehead you gently received,
most eminently, my scream, and guarded
to the depths of my affection,
long been unwhetted

and I bless your sweet eyes
that trespassed over the cobweb shield
I muse behind, and I send you
off without your knowing
of your having my tenderness revitalized,
and brushing on my colored day

7

this morning a wisdom
called upon me as he does
and I awoke this morning
not when rising out of
my bed,
I did not sleep at all
last night and
this fine morning is my own...

and once I am elated
from a spark rained
to me, and kissed my
palm,–Faith gloriously,
and I asked him if this is
right, or that, and about this
place when I feel no where...
he replied most faithfully
"Elude yourself from there"

8

and do not commit me
to you for I will spoil
away like a fine wine uncapped,
and untapped forever
will I contain a quality
pure and forbidden as the watery sea, no man can expect
to cup into his hands and
taste and accept, and for you the
breath of my countenance and the static
of my eyes will expire,
(and I will burn out)
bless me for not being won so easily---
— I, intangible—

9

morning not so early
noon is almost there
the tines of sun, they break out
everyday a topaz hair
the morning is late now, and I'm
to go out walking,
my step is somewhat jovial
while my presence is unlocking
enarmoured, I, and fierceless
although my day is late
I have joined the Scotts for coffee
to give my breath a bate

10 SPRINGTIME MAGNOLIA.

there will come a time soon,
        no doubt, that you will
be removed from my mind

        and when the spring
magnolia trees break open their
tulip flowers I will remember
how much you felt for that springing foliage

        there will come a time
when no doubt will
play upon the reigns
of my heart, and no regret
that you aren't different or any
hope that you may change because
you are indifferent, indifferent to
the sea, to the sky and to
the spirit that breathes inside you.

and I muse over your
affection for me, which was
not constant–with lack of
respect for that untamed, vital
substance which made me–**me**,
and that part of me you loved
and tried to strangle–I could
go on and on about that
but what is ultimately frustrating
is that you cannot perceive the true nature of man, now...
        so shallow are you

there are thousands of men
sucked hollow, presiding over
the earth like empty shells
for they are beautiful even
when broken, but they do not
contain
the essence, the fibre

and now I shift out
to view again the little daisies
that surprise the grass–if you
were here I would make you a chain to wear on your gentle
head to smile on those tender
eyes of yours that had a certain
setting of olive skin glow.

it's silly to ponder upon you
when you are not here and maybe
never really close to my
mind, bound to my will

you are as endless as the rillling
sea, just a wave that once
grasped my life and shook me,
one water I will never forget...

But I am younger now
and stronger...I only hope
that you enjoy this magnolia day.

11

and I sit here wistfully for you
dreading the thought of hearing your truck
door slam and the jingle of your dog's
copper collar and tags
and your demanding footsteps
and overruling presence
and overbearing attitude

oh, how if I were at a
vista where I could watch
you when I was bored with the
rest of the world...I would reach
out my sun rays and warm your
shoulders and sweet eyelids, trying

to tell you that this is your
morning
and the spring without you
sheds cherry blossom tears that
bruise by the warm wind
and wear away as I
steady myself on the ground
and hold my head high
and try to fantasy away
my nightly hours before retiring
but my lids are too heavy

and it would only be a drudgery for me
to think of you

12

the trial of spring brings
to mind there must be
a constant to overmind
the meaningless behavior of
the human being. A center
to which the paradox of life
ceases to become a mystery and
the worldly condition is a positive attribute.

though how horrid and
unjust the organization that man
has accepted on this planet,
it is one of the trivial
points of space and affects not the
whole, except for without earth
the universe would not be the whole...

13

I am a plastered vagabond
of vagabondancy I am enscounced
and I live a good clean life
where disorder is pronounced

I lay a claim to slovenry,
excitement and to chance
I do decree an heavenry
of disarray and dance!

14

        if there's near, no far can there be
if only near we choose to see
        but if it's barely near we see
then more closely far can be
        and if it's mostly far we see
then more further near will be
if neither near nor far is there
best we make it to the closest bar
(and sap at random the nearest par)

15

how funny i am to see
your funnier showing
        and laughing i had a line there
   trying though, upside down
   too bad, and
        it scurried like rabbits
   flurried the white block ink race
   and buried forever itself
        of obsidian spread
            in ink brink day

16

impatience and impervity
impel and impart
a play in diversity
the subversity of art
imperative and impersonal
are proclaims of our kind
who don't properly present
their protrusion in behind
may this be a problem
or pointless to rename
i'd be compelled to have them propelled
if better were my aim

17

What I find most often lacking
is a self-instructed backing
absence of the vital bone
constitutes the common drone

being without quality
is the statement of most humanoid
examples of humanity
who with life's cement construct a void

I tell my friends, so few and fine
that those of substance not of spine
are not worth the paying heed
and are betraying when we need

be proud for being arrogant
eccentric and yet humble!
your will holds content that their's can't
for in no will they will crumble

I find the soullessness of a machine
is to what he tends to lean
but enough of them! only recognize
those whom you may 'oft despise

and those who are real
will shed their guise
for those with a head
do not shade their eyes

18

today the season
serene in tonal air of green
a flash that blushed my
eyes one morning
reminded me of the truth that is me

19

the sun it is disclosing
and i am in pain
to fill my eyes of blueness
that soon will not remain

and though i am saddened
i find something revealing
oh, it is the evening
its steady lid unpeeling

and night, he restless rustles
turning at the stroke
of a ceasing day of bustles
the seal of day has broke

and every dusk it happens
the evening is renewed
when sun melts the horizon
the nighteye is unglued

20

shall you belittle me
if little shall i be

if little mean you whittle
then whittle on a tree

if little then mean you be-laugh at me
then laugh at me and be

laugh then for a little while
for your mouth can hold a sea

21

i've decided that i want to be
a tutor of the common flea
when a flea becomes a hag
she is named a flea bag

when one decides to beat a flea
he will then put on his mitten
one will win a victory
while the other ends up flea-bitten

some of them have little hair
some of their hair is greasy
some of them are completely bare
while others are quite fleasy

some of them have a car
but have trouble trying to park-it
but it's worth when the travel far
to visit the flea market

we humans think we've got things rough
our troubles are mainly ones with ants
don't you think dogs have had enough
when they have fleas in their pants?

when people think i'm dumb, i sneer
and beg for their apology
and leave them with a flea in the ear
for my astuteness in fleology!

22

sun waits at your window
your eyes fold into your pillow
the dew it is a frosting
moon becomes a willow

waken to the morning
your hand it is a thread
wind shakes the night-time
from its lightened head

23

that satisfies me!
(write that down for further reference
and despite of deference)

that satisfies me!
and i repeat the sound
pleases me... oh how
i'm glad i'm not a cow
and i will not bow now
to the single plow
written to harness
and harass my
mind is not an ass!

24

yesterday i was made of pencils
today i am molasses
and before i was a piece of steel
kicking people's asses

someday i will be a glob
grinning my defeat
now i write a syrupy day
tempered by the heat

25

must it be that my witticisms
arouse in you such criticisms?

that one could only be so vain
as to indulge in others' mental pain
by so blatantly lacking wit
as to cause one's humor to quit!

    i say then!...let their faces fall!
best be misunderstood, then to utter drawl.

26

    may you ask me not to be a fool
then may you ask me not to be wise

    may you criticize and test my wit
then may you teach me to despise

    may you ask me to contain myself
lest i reveal your private dreams

    then mayn't the jester be
    less the clown he seems?

the cottonwood are tiny puffs
that speckle in the air
little tuffs that drift and sail
on wings of angel hair

Cottonwood

the cottonwood are little puffs
that infiltrate the skies
little strings of thready stuffs
that gooey up my eyes!

Cottonwood II

POEMS

ALTER EGO

What curious happenstance
made me appear in a dream?
Love letters to thrill a woman's spirit
if you knew me as a chance
to tap your artistic stream
my folly is waiting to hear it

by your nature you must oppose
a suspect-artist having philandered
perhaps jealous of talents possessed
understandable to have chose
one incompatible with your standard
through needing to be caressed

the truth will dissolve the thread
two gypsy beings held
I'll turn myself inside out to show you that I could never be wed
to whom I am meld...
Though I have loved my Alter Ego

BEAUTIFUL DAY FOR FALLING IN LOVE

How could it be such a beautiful morning?
how could there be magical light
Light transcends the waking city
Light drapes the dazzling air

I am fighting a descent from heaven
how can you speak of normal things--
all talk of daily chores and such
doth rob my powered wings!

Silence!..perhaps you do not understand
that **I** keeps **me** apart
to wander the limitless range of love
guided by an adventurous heart

So, please enjoy the silence wherein
this passion of mine dwells
and only dare to distract me with kisses
to refill these hungerous wells

Riding the swift cloud of scents, feelings, tastes, touches
and of a spirit free
Steal not!----I offer to share the silence with thee!

BEST FRIENDS

Do you ever wonder how profound
When you feel low they gather 'round!
And about all the many dreary days
They have soothed–cheered–listened–with their furry ways!

Let us be watchful of **their** sufferings too
For they lack a human voice, unlike me and you
They might tell us by a head held low
They might hide away or more affection show.

As Caretakers let us be wise
And learn to read the messages in their eyes
Let us take care of them and we will have no regrets
When we are kind servants to our pets!

BUTTERFLY

My dear, my gypsy
we have taught ourselves how not to stray
Adulthood, the Sentinel

In Time's design that we align
to be a butterfly is my task
will you help me, my Dear?

Please be a butterfly with me!

COTTONWOOD (1972)

the cottonwood are tiny puffs
that speckle in the air
little tuffs that drift and sail
on wings of angel hair

and woodpeckers, their may-poled dance
pretending to be shy
have barely time to spare a glance
to the bluing sky

the wind is sweet with cotton stuffs
and gustfully it billows
so that the stars may air the bluffs
of their fluffy pillows

COTTONWOOD 11 (1985)

the cottonwood are little puffs
that infiltrate the skies!
little strings of cotton stuff
that gooey up my eyes!

what makes these little wispy fluffs
attach themselves to my eyeballs
I must say–I've had enough!
they must know they have no rivals!

they cause me to blink and itch
and then my eyes get redder
they find my nose, it starts to twitch
which doesn't feel any better!

mosquitoes don't cause my pen to flow
and my nose too, it is itchy so
as for the havoc that **they** cause
I can write many a flowery clause!

DAVID OF MY DREAMS

Could I have met one kindred, dear
who kissed the jasmine behind my ear?
An art gallery–the setting, one hour's time
has set this girl's heart a'rhyme

How could I have charmed you so?
In books any story is fair
I need not know how or why
I abide to Romance's dare

You are unafraid–amazement I adore!

The bird of sunshine has found my palm
It dips its wings in all things
In flight it sparkles the air and trees
In water it gleams

Your pretty eyes I've seen

David of my dreams
I have heard you listening to me
When I spoke you were a mirror
Tell me, what do you see?

HAIR (THE)

It was at the Great Falls Jazz festival
on a temporary job–I was serving cocktails
I am always on the lookout for romance
and there was Larry...he sure could dance!

The psychic selling CD's said Larry is single
I said "Well, I'll drop my cocktail napkins near him, we'll mingle"
but I didn't go through with it–she called me chicken
but I thought Larry was weird, and the routine was hick'n

And looking at Larry, who having elegance and grace
attire a cut above anyone else in the place
filled my romantic designs with despair
it isn't–well, anything...BUT..WELL...THE HAIR!!

I don't think Larry would mind if I critiqued his hairdo
how it fits in Montana, I haven't a clue
but I finally figured out where his arrangement would fly
in a rock band...or more!..YES. A movie!!..SCI-FI!

But to me it's like Larry is of an odd race
better yet, maybe outer space
like I say–to kids his do might make the girls drool
and start a fad with guys in school..SUPER COOL!

But watching Larry sip cranberry juice with elegant posture
I could not enlist him on my conquest roster
But he eyed me like I might be a prospective morsel
and we danced after my shift on the dance floorsel

And last Friday I ran into Kathy who had visited Larry in Kalispell
she said Larry's harmless and eccentric as well
so if he wonders who is to blame for this witty
well, I guess our talking about him inspired this ditty

So, I have decided that if I marry Larr
He'll have to sign a pre-nuptial agreement to alter his hair
I've already chosen a stylist I can trust to change it
but would Larry honor this legal arrangement?

But I feel an insight coming to me with this thing with the hair
Larry's looking for a woman whom he won't scare!!
You know the story, Beauty and the Beast, Phantom of the OP'
just came up with a new title.. "Love Surpassed Larry's Mop"!!

So when Larry finds her he'll drop the hairade and go hip
sandals, a beard, maybe a mustache o'er his lip
on the dance floor hair flying he'll be a fine sight to gazer
in white slacks, beads, headband and kelly green blazer!

LOVER OF SUNSETS

Surroundant of warmth
that voice has found me
as we are yet of youthful body
and did not have to wait until aging needs to be taken gracefully

Lover of Sunsets
I am in that dream and you are in that dream
fearless of love
the only true courage and bravery
is the heart offered and begged to be taken

Lover of Sunsets
not afraid to drench yourself of passions
and what, my Dear, is **your** favorite sunset?

Is it a violent rash of screaming reds that leaden the sky maybe
with some painful orange and yellows too dramatic to view for
very long that they need to soften so that the eye will not perish
from their throbbing beauty?

Is it the pinks and lavenders with fine white wisps in artificial
arrangements like a children's storybook?

Could your favorite be a coal-gray sunset with wet round clouds
broken by two rainbows?

Have you seen three different sunsets in the sky when it might be
hard to know where the sun really is if you didn't know where it
was **supposed** to be
that was MY favorite...when I was alone and tired

what a sad joy to see these things with only one pair of eyes
LOVER OF SUNSETS

PATH OF PAIN

If only the heart could test how fate unravels
before its journey is about to begin
so it may not choose the Path of Pain for its travels
and for **no** happiness, one could choose to win

I'd rather have the freedom of bliss
than the woes to share with womankind
and the sorrow would be okay to miss
my spirit need not to hurt to not be blind

PATTY IN ITALY

Patty, I'm sure we all envy you
if, for nothing else, you're doing something new.
Most of us will continue our same life styles
while you're away in Milan, some 5,767 air miles.
We all must wonder in our own ways
how Patty in Italy will be spending her days!

Do students bring apples or strings of garlic to the teachas?
To be mean, do they throw meatballs or pizzas?

What is the Italian word for "skeet"?
How do say "pull"? how so you say "OH SH_ _ DARNEET!"?

We all know Italians are famous for distributing pinches,
will you soften these blows by putting on inches?
Will your new friends think that your buns are too bony
and in their concern, feed you tons of spumoni?
They might think your buttocks need to be meaty
and urge you to cultivate a bigger seaty,
and how will all this affect your game of skeety?
Will an overweight Patty admit or deny it
when Margie tells her she needs the Cambridge Diet?

I'm sure all of us girls are curious
and wonder about things which may or may not be injurious.
For instance, do Italian women let their hair grow on their legs and armpits?
If you do this, will it turn Gary on, or give him the fits?
And when you come back to the USA will anyone stare?
Will they pity poor Patty with her plump derriere?

Patty, I hope you don't take offense to this ditty
with all my dwelling on the place where you sh—sitty.
But, tell me this, have you purchased a padded girdle for your bottom?
If not, try Frederick's of Hollywood, I know they've got 'em.
Do you think slapping a pincher is permitted?

Is there punishment for this?.. has a crime been committed?
It seems like such and odd custom!
Boy...! if someone tweaked **my** butt, I'd sure like to bust 'em!

Just think...isn't it uncanny!
A nation's fixation aimed at a fanny!
It's asstounding a people would raise such a fuss
over a gluteal maximus!
Think of all the time and energy they spend
in adulation over the rear end!
Patty,–you better wear a badge on your tush to remind
stating, "I SHOT 2,000 STRAIT----HANDS OFF MY BEHIND!!!!

One last question, Patty,
do you think it will bruise, callous or bleester?
Never mind, Patty, we envy you, **but not your keister!**

SALESMAN (THE)

I was ambitious, fed up with life
and ready to overcome my poverty and strife.
So, I wandered to the big city of Billings
certain to make many financial killings.

I decided that I must learn from a master
so I could make my fortune must faster.
I sought out the champion of sales, known as "The Monolith".
Yes, my life changed, I met Mr. Harry Myth.

Myth taught **"**...this may not be as hard as you think.
You're rash if you think I'm a typical fink.
Young mothers and others will be tickled pink
if you follow my method–a 'Squeeze and a Wink'.

The squeeze is placed on the arm or the shoulder
and it works on those persons who are younger or older.
Then you throw in a wink when your feeling bolder
and before you can say 'Squink'–you've sold 'er!

Pay attention now, you must never pinch
or your customer's wallet won't budge an inch.
It's not hard to make the deal clinch,
I'm living proof that the **Squeeze** is a cinch.

Now, there's nothing more charming to folks than a **Wink**.
It warms men like success and women like mink.
Now you say--doesn't this theory have at least one kink?
Why! It will bring your fortune right up to the brink!

Remember though, there is a wink, and then there is a **Wink!**
You don't want to make your customers shrink
and it must be more than a casual blink
They can always spot one that's rinky dink.

Never underestimate the power of a Squinkle
it's a sure way to abolish a frown or a wrinkle.
Customers hand you their money while their eyes twinkle,
even the skies open up to let money tinkle!"

Yes, I sure learned my lesson from Harry.
I sold more cars than a dealer could carry
but my health is gone now as I sit here thinking
how my arms and eyes wore out from a lifetime of Squinking!

YOUR FIRST SURRENDER

Cupid has no reasons
he is just fulfilling fate
no riddles, passwords, tasks or rhymes
he leaves just an open gate

You asked me what was happening
as the sun moved 'oer Earth's brow
our soul-to-soul was interlacing
in that placing known as "NOW"

you've not shown me where your heart lives
but you let me lead you to the home of mine
one knows beyond feeling when one totally gives
that which language cannot define

I replied it was love we were making
that was partly true
in your giving I was taking
Your First Surrender from you

06/06/02

I am the ocean across the table
your eyes draw me to the shore of your being
I cannot believe the feelings I am drenched in
I cannot believe the power with the man I am seeing

There is nothing but this moment's heady animation
two strangers who have decided to meet
I know you, too, are immersed in this creation
locked in a stare we break a quick glance to the street

This is Chapter 1, I am suspended
I cannot hope or dream that this will last
perhaps it has already ended
and all this amazement will have boldly passed

08/28/00

The soundless music, I can hear it
flowing in and through my spirit
though I do not understand
I feel it gently tug my hand

I have no choice but to take its lead
for there is something that I need

and it does not promise me no pain
but to remove me from the mundane

for in following I shall be alive
to sputter, whirl, ascend and dive

no calm or safety nor one to share
love is the prize

don't ask me yet, just now–just listen
see the seconds, how they glisten!
Time has stopped and dances near
and is caught between our breathing

UNTITLED

The wind rolled down through the icy sea
And tossed the turbulent waves toward me
The sea thrust forth it's forest green weed
The sea, the womb of the first born seed
A race with the foam, struggle with the current
Confusion of what the great Neptune meant
When he emerged from the depths shaking his curls so vain
And then pierced the water, his star-topped cane

His amused roar was the ocean, his laugh was the foam
Like leaf on a tree, a snail in its home
The water swerved around and over the ancient boulders
And Neptune, hiding, only shrugged his great shoulders.

UNTITLED (written at age fourteen)

Lo, for the sun that
shines in the summer
Lo, for the creek in its
muted mummer
Lo, for Joy in the morning
will shine and sing
The bells, a sunset that
often cling
Lo, for the frisky happy dogs
The baby laughs as it jogs
Lo, for the sun the mist
doth screen
Lo, for the girl, the girl
fourteen!